Chimayó is a census-designated place (CDP) in Rio Arriba and Santa Fe counties in New Mexico. The name derives from Tewa for a local landmark, the hill of Tsi Mayoh. The CDP is unincorporated and includes many neighborhoods, called plazas or placitas, each with its own name, including El Potrero de Chimayó—the plaza near Chimayó's communal pasture—and the Plaza del Cerro—plaza by the hill. The cluster of plazas called Chimayó lies near Santa Cruz, about 25 miles north of Santa Fe. The deciduous trees that lie in this area down from the rocky terrain hills that surround the CDP all seem to have weather sculpted cruelty dug into their bark that seems more like a gallery than a place for shade.

The Trees Of Chimayó

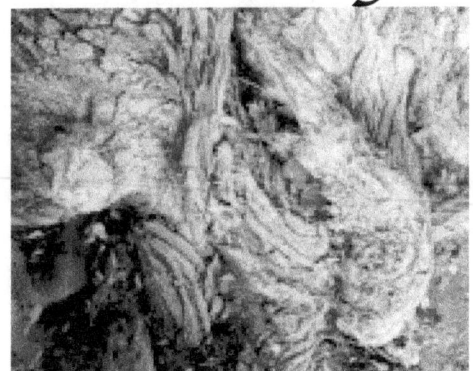

Photographs
By
David Cope

The Trees of Chimayo
Photographs by David Cope

Epoc Books
Printed in the United States of America
© David Cope 2016
All Rights Reserved.
Published 2012.

This book is dedicated to my wife, sons, and grandchildren, Zoe, Tess, Gavin, and Ethan whose excitement for everyday things never ceases to amaze me. And to those older kids like me who believe in those children.

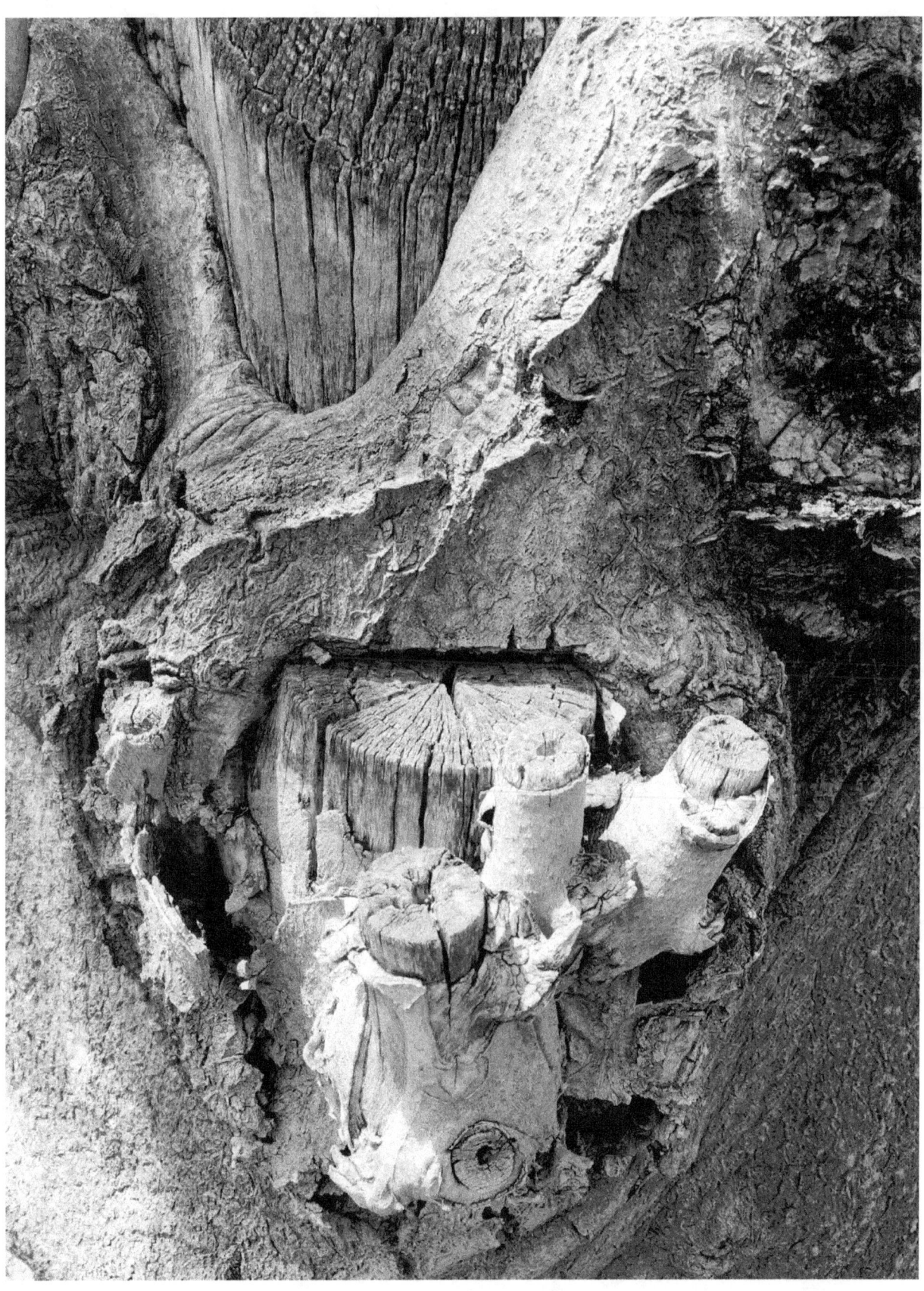

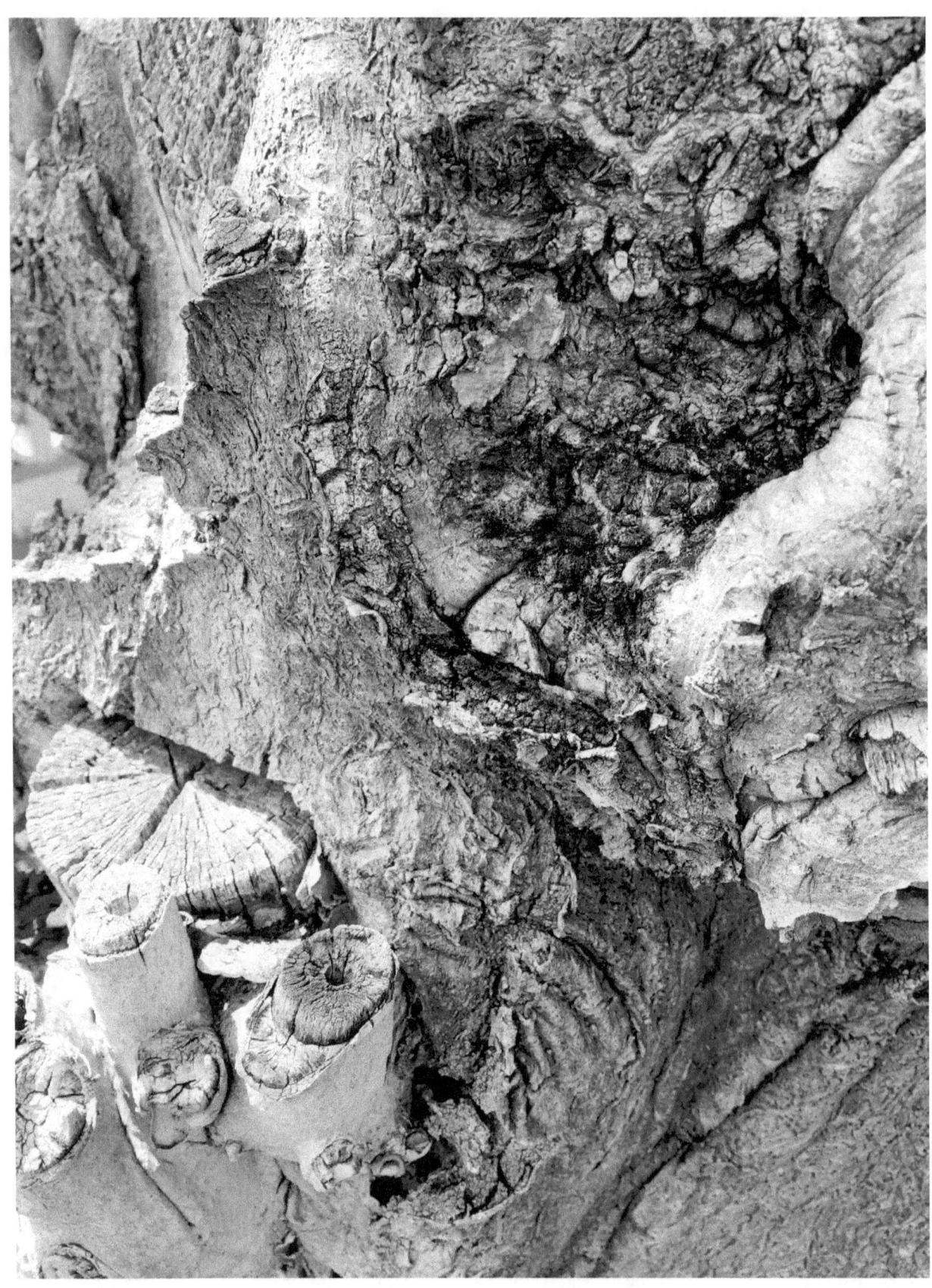

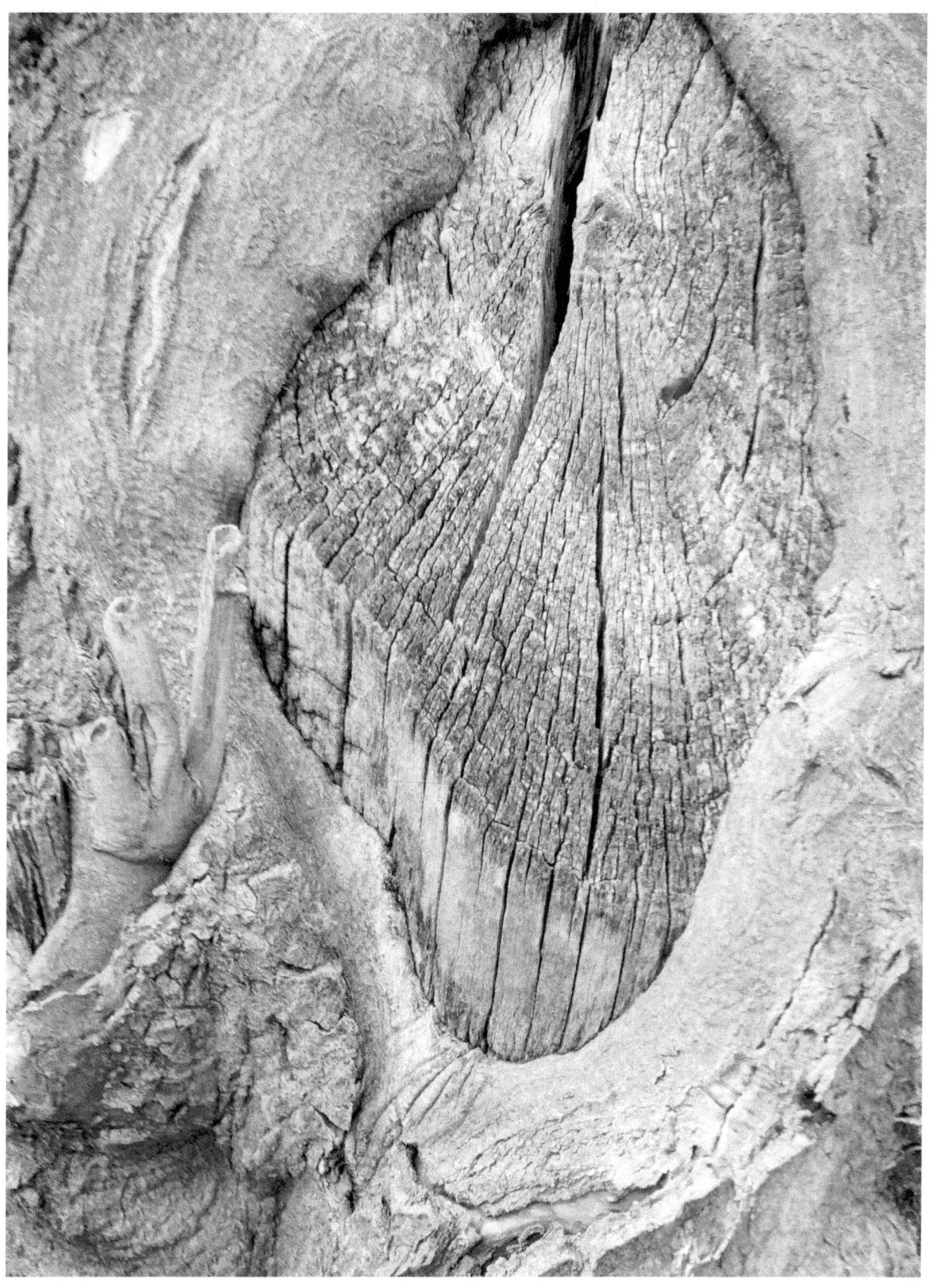

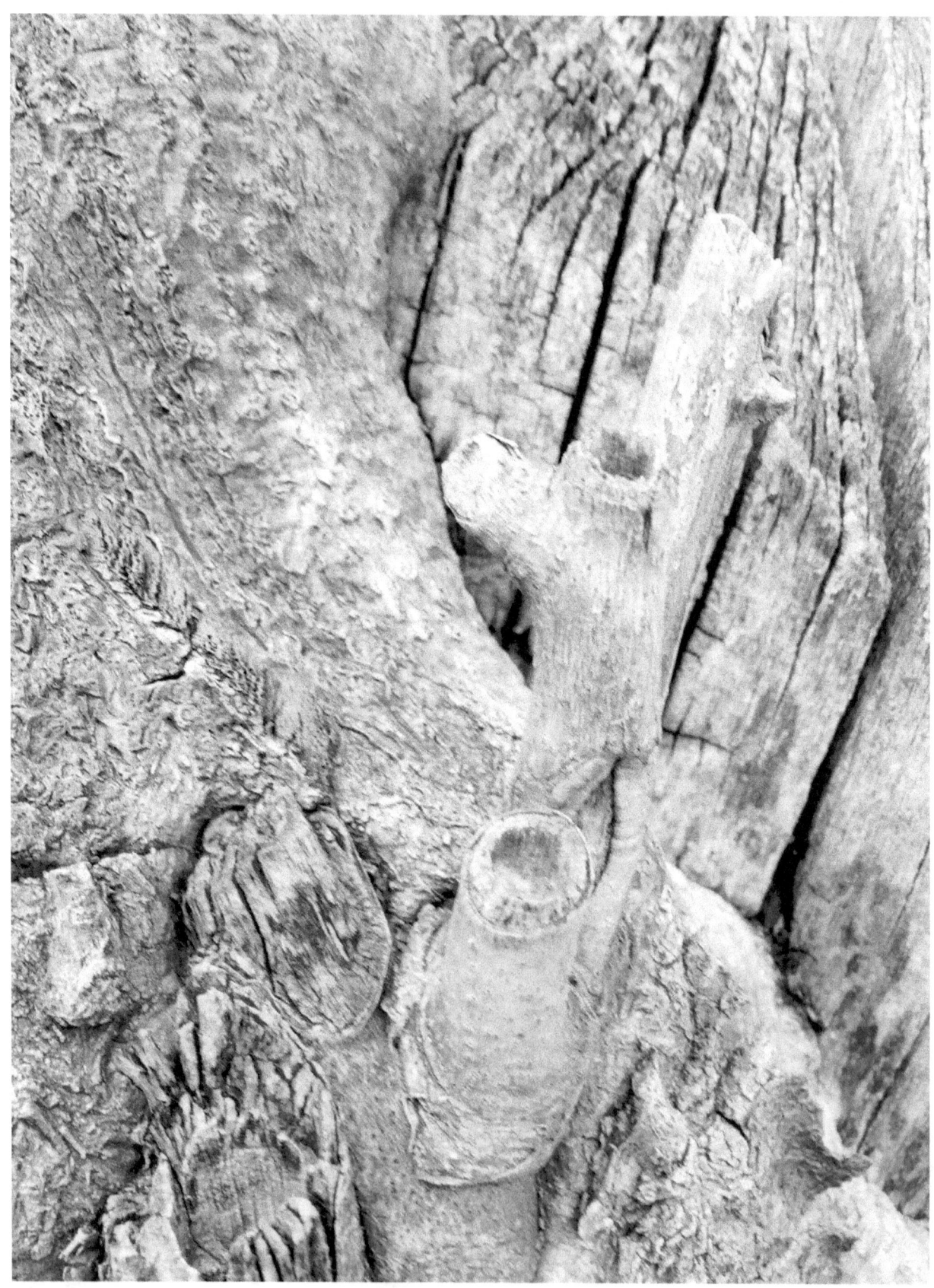

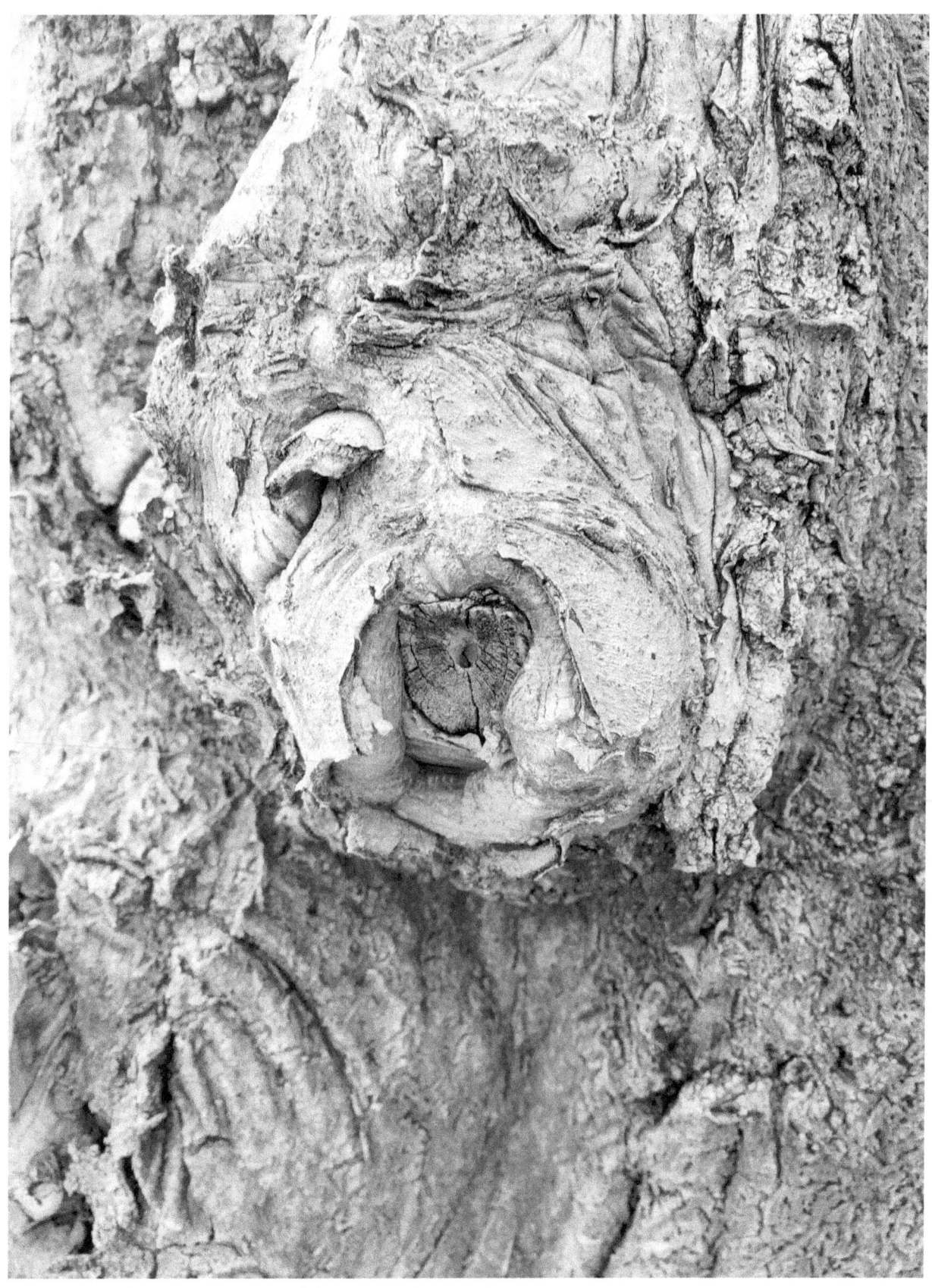

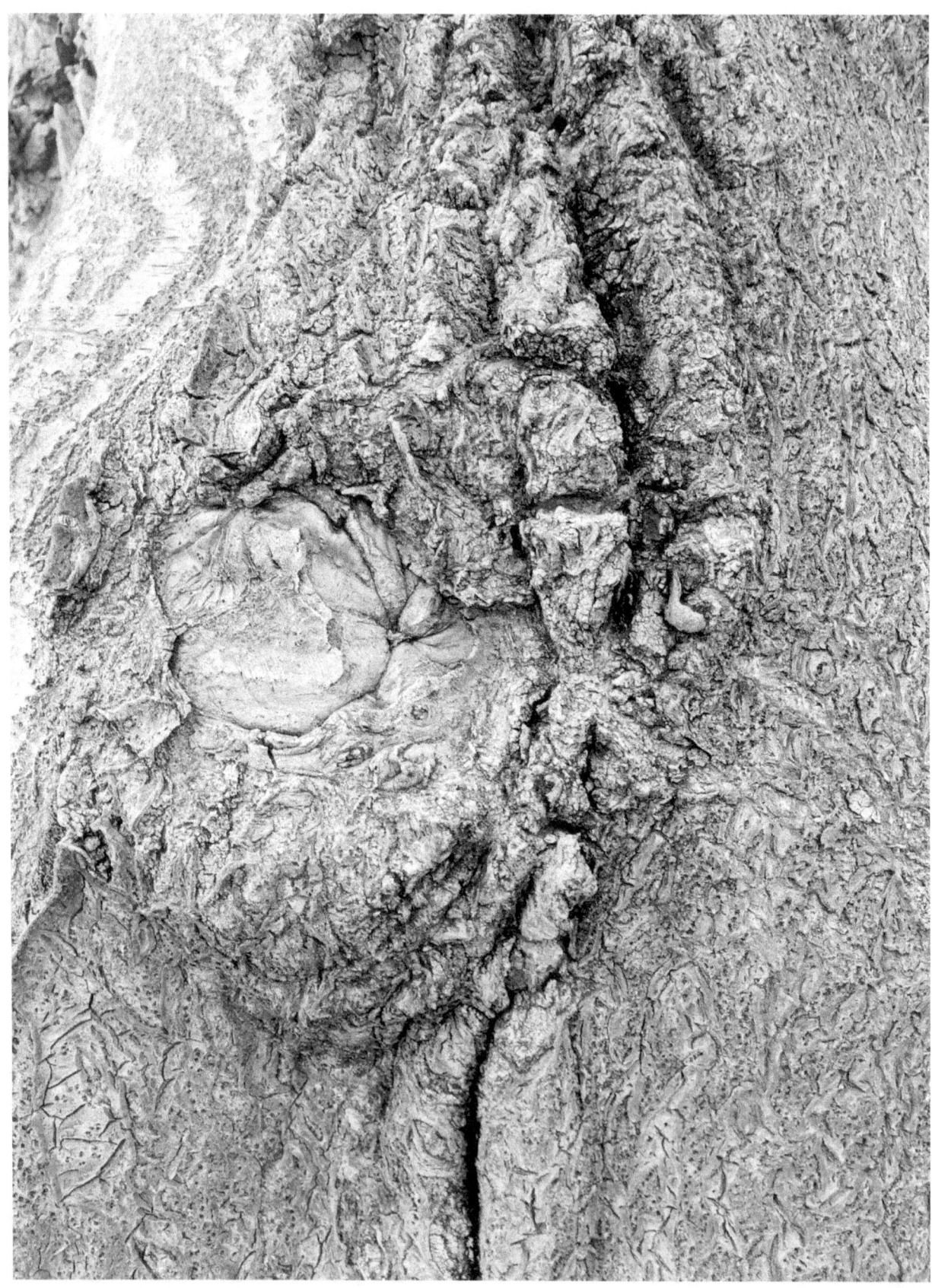

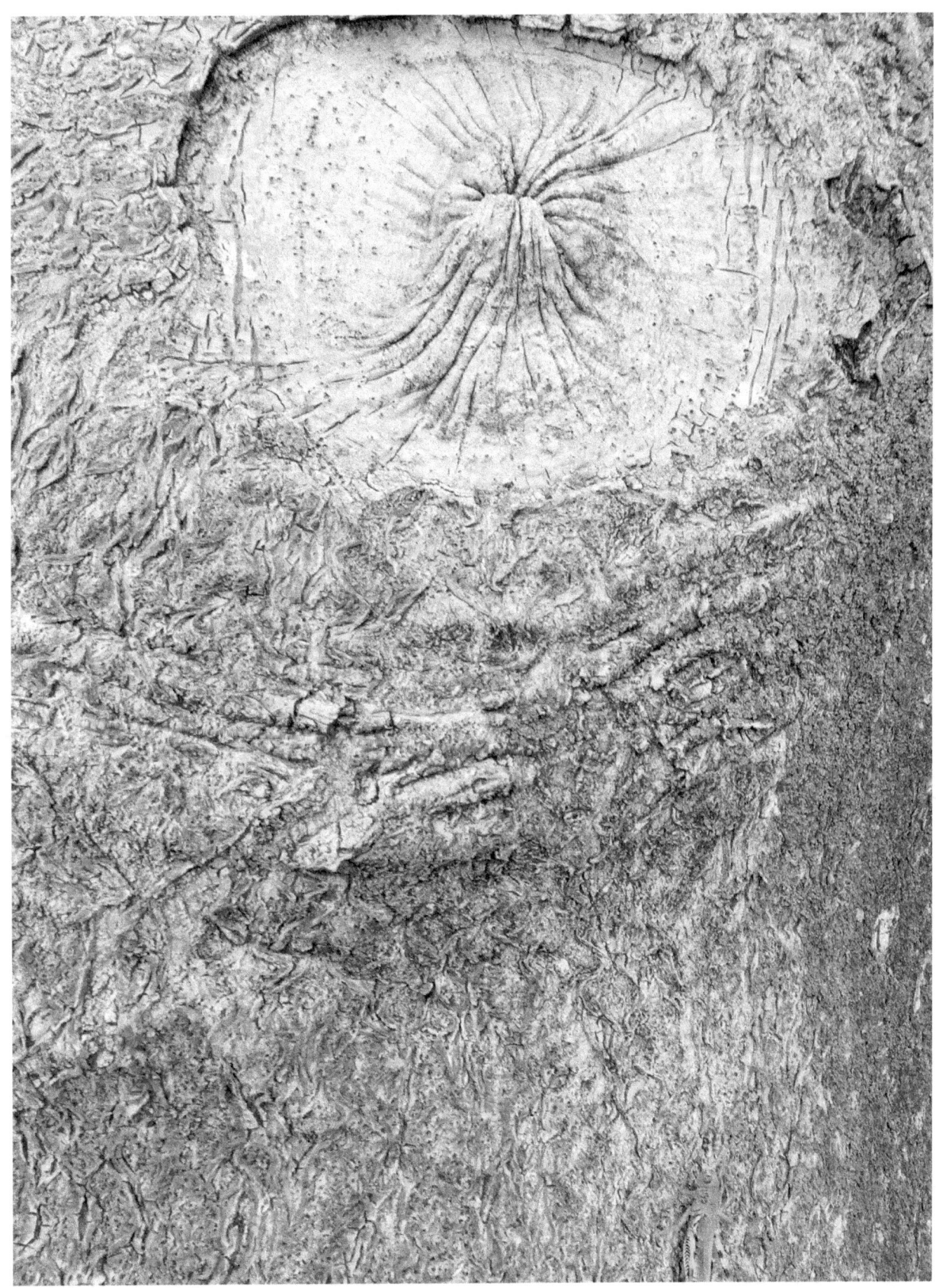

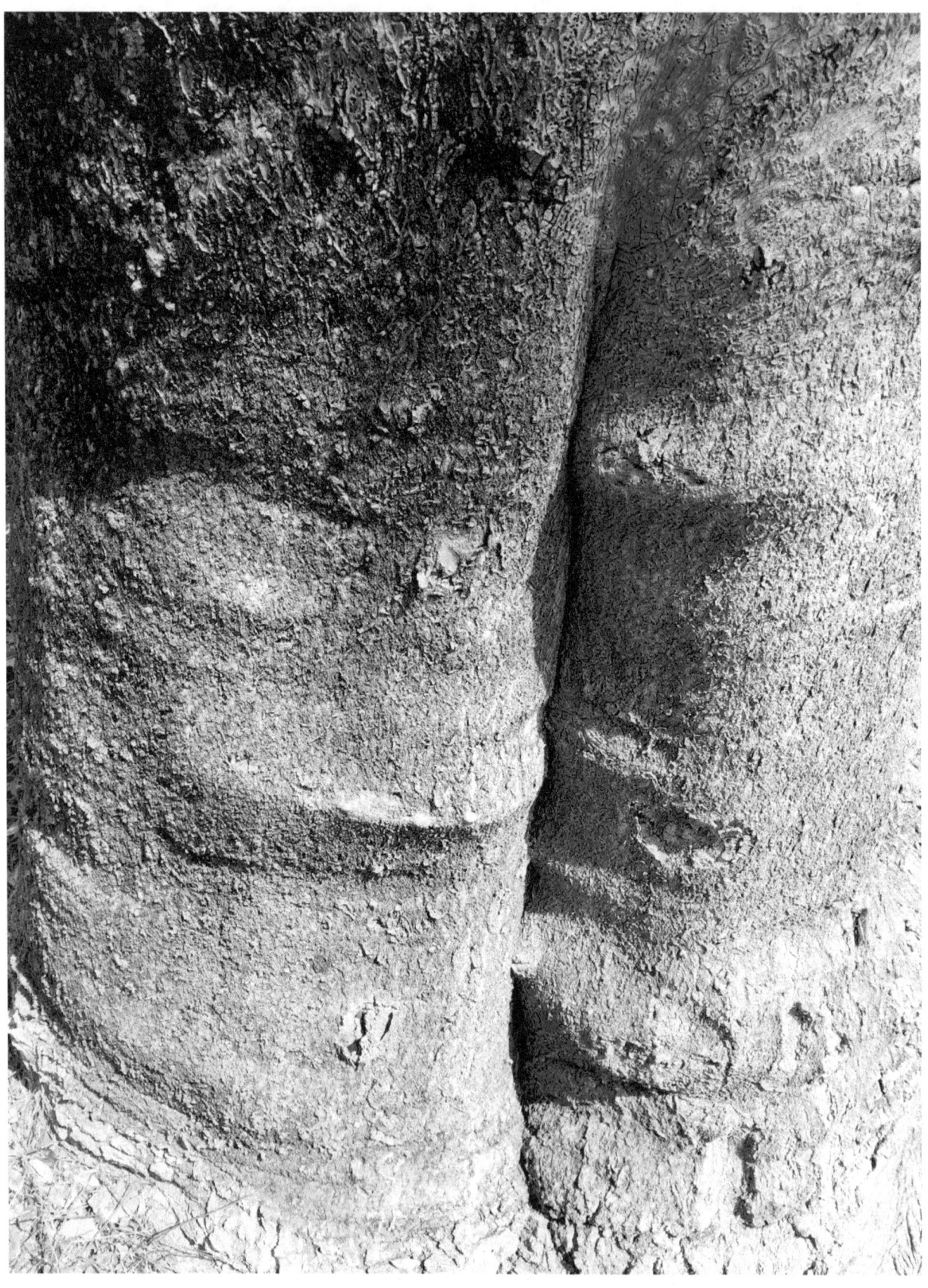

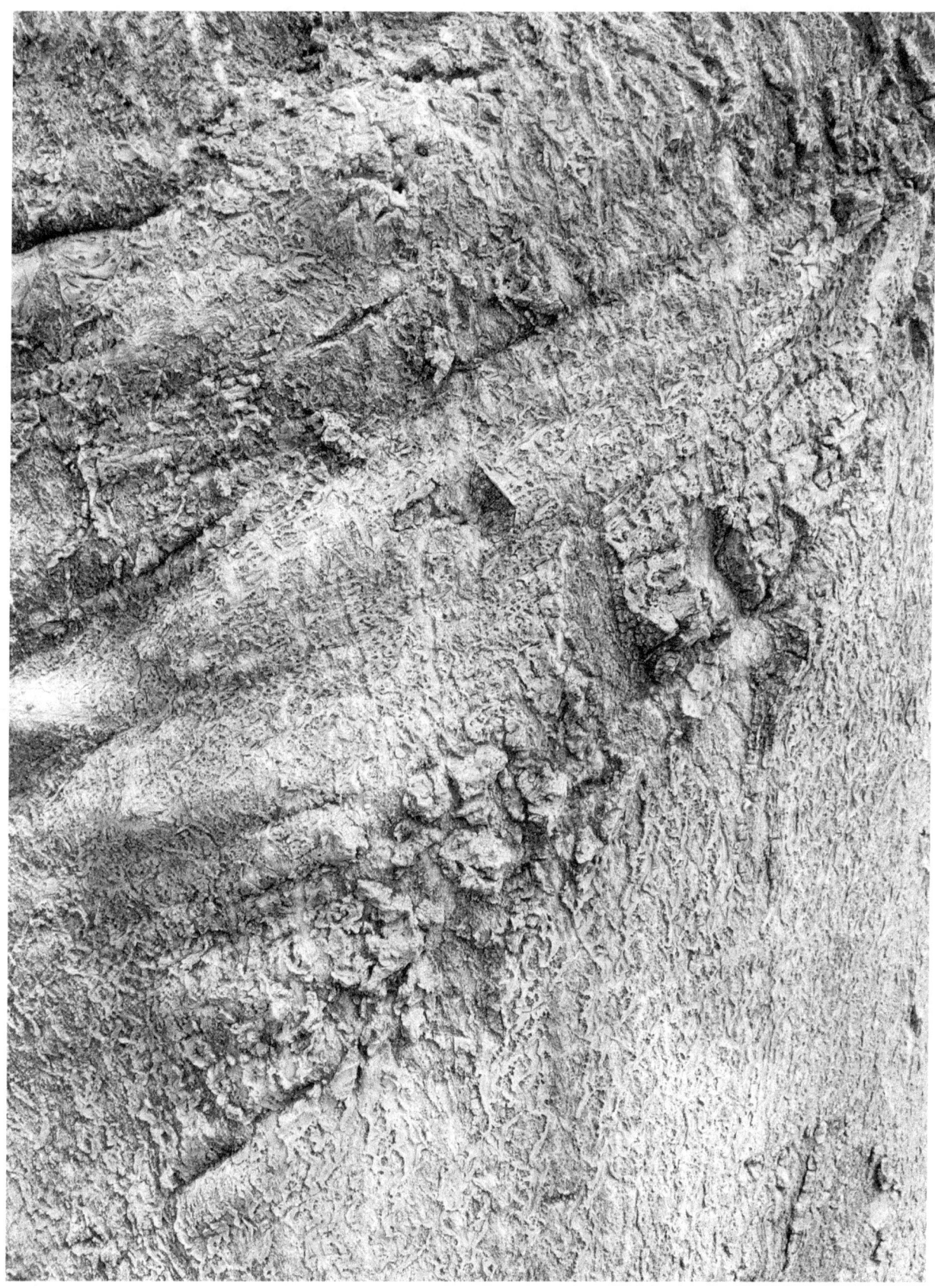

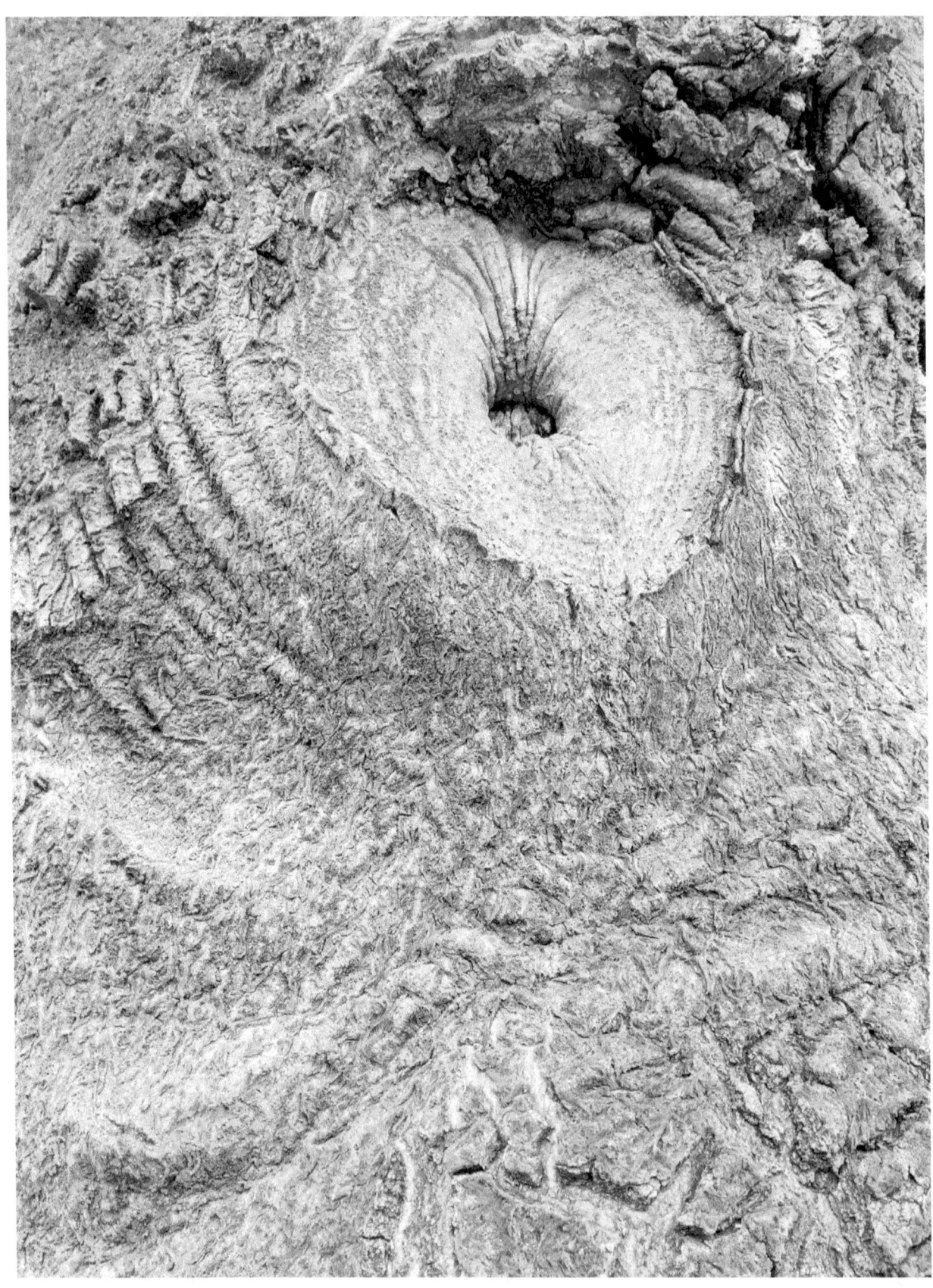

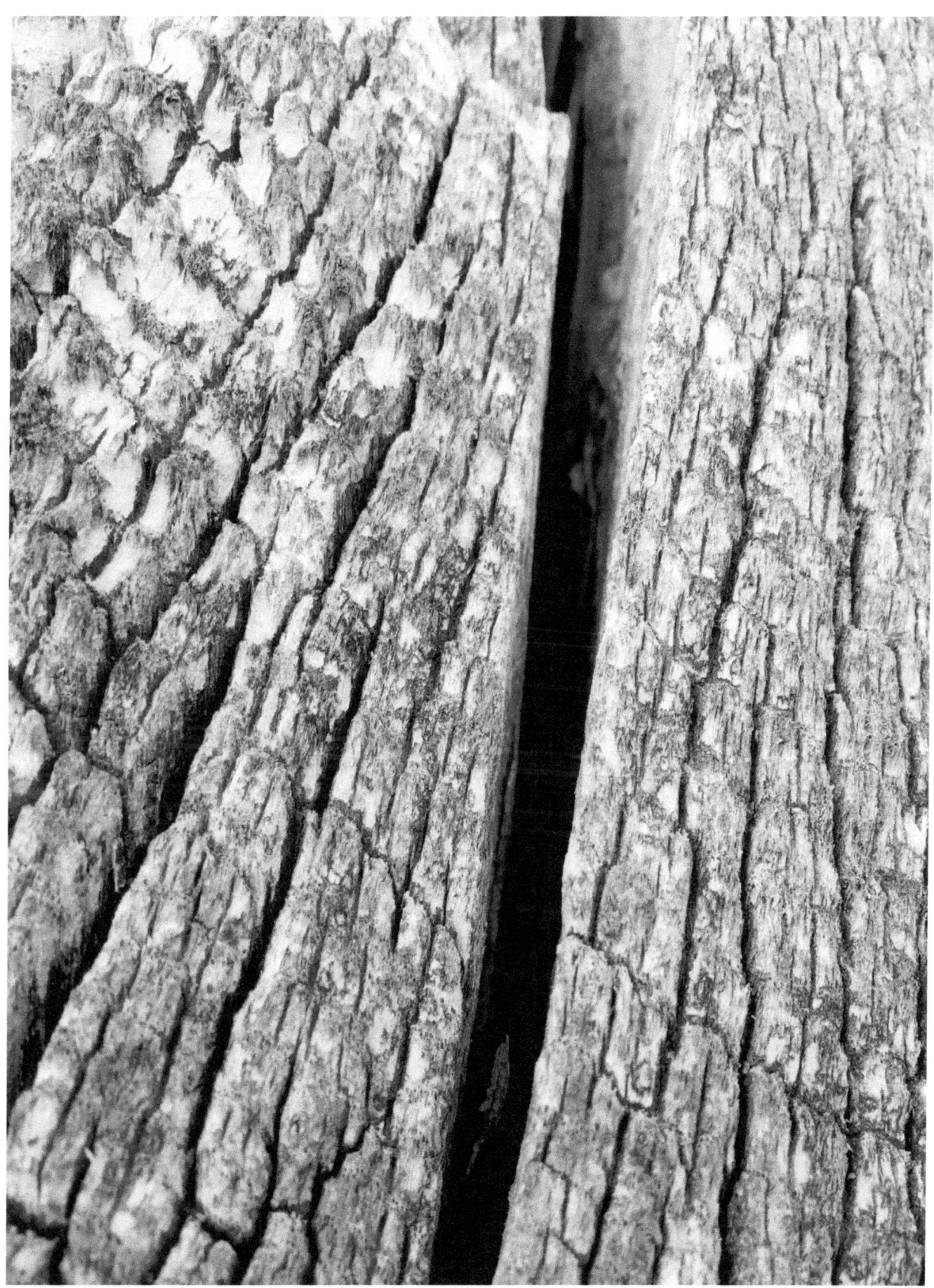

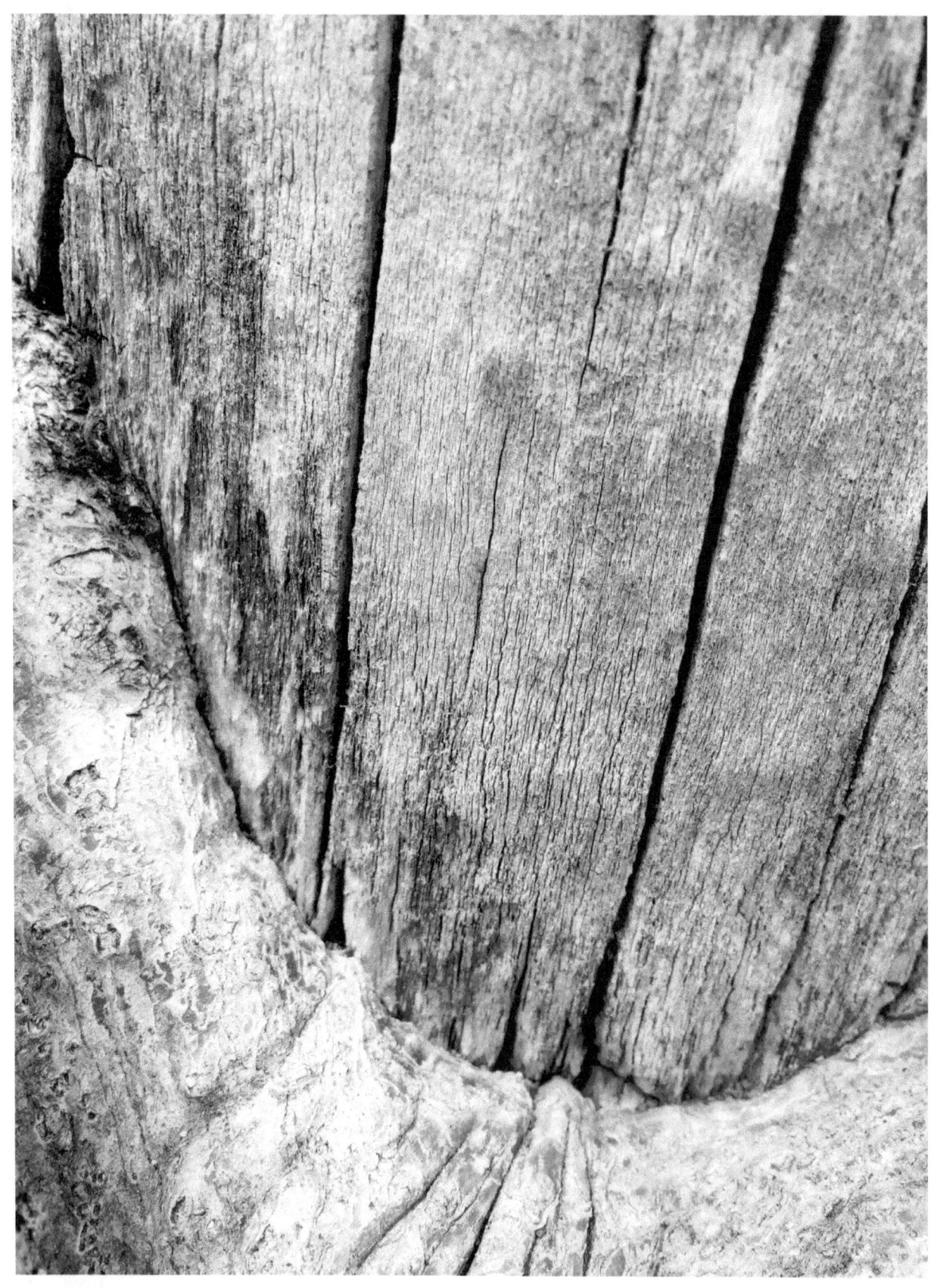

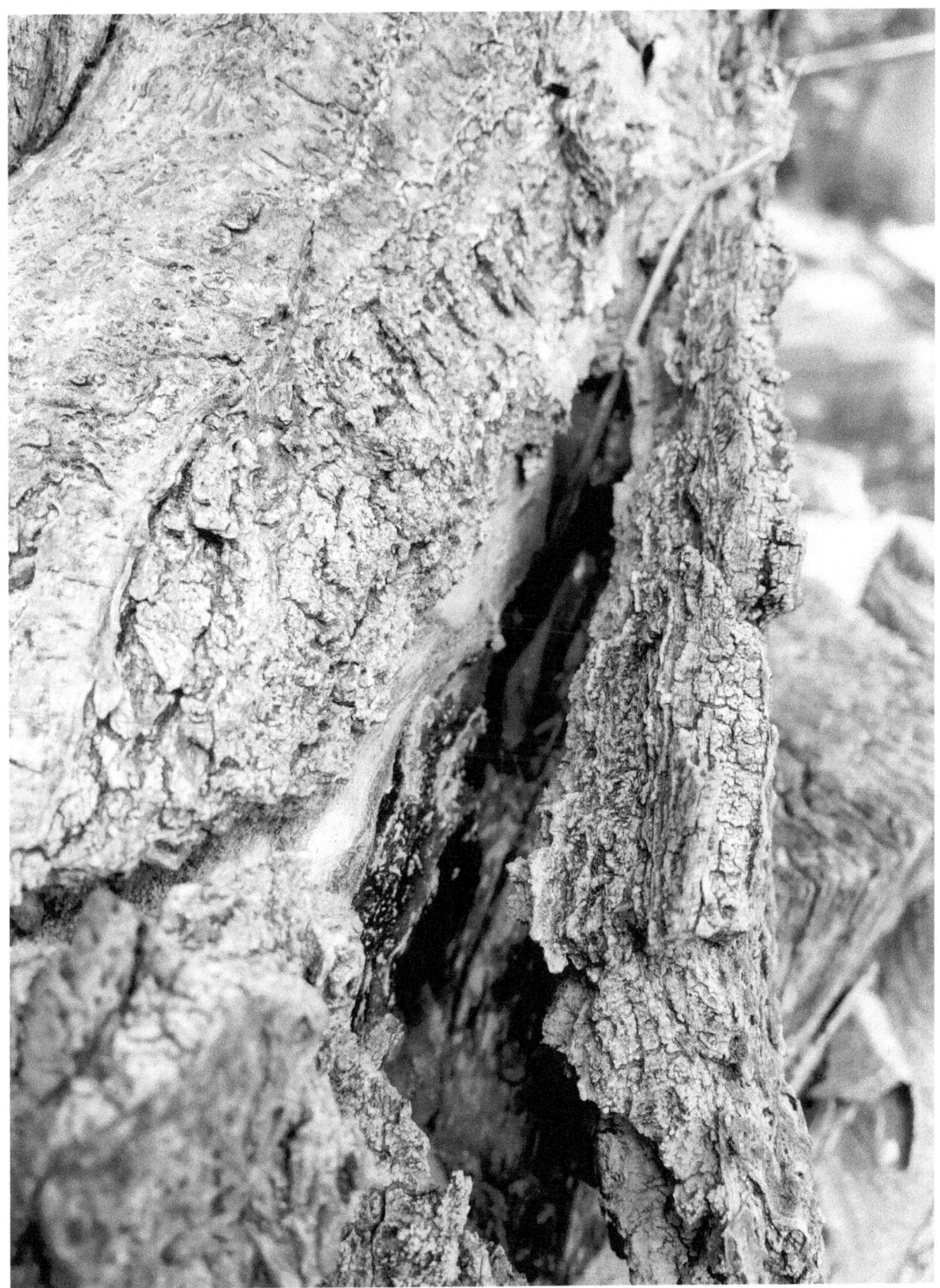

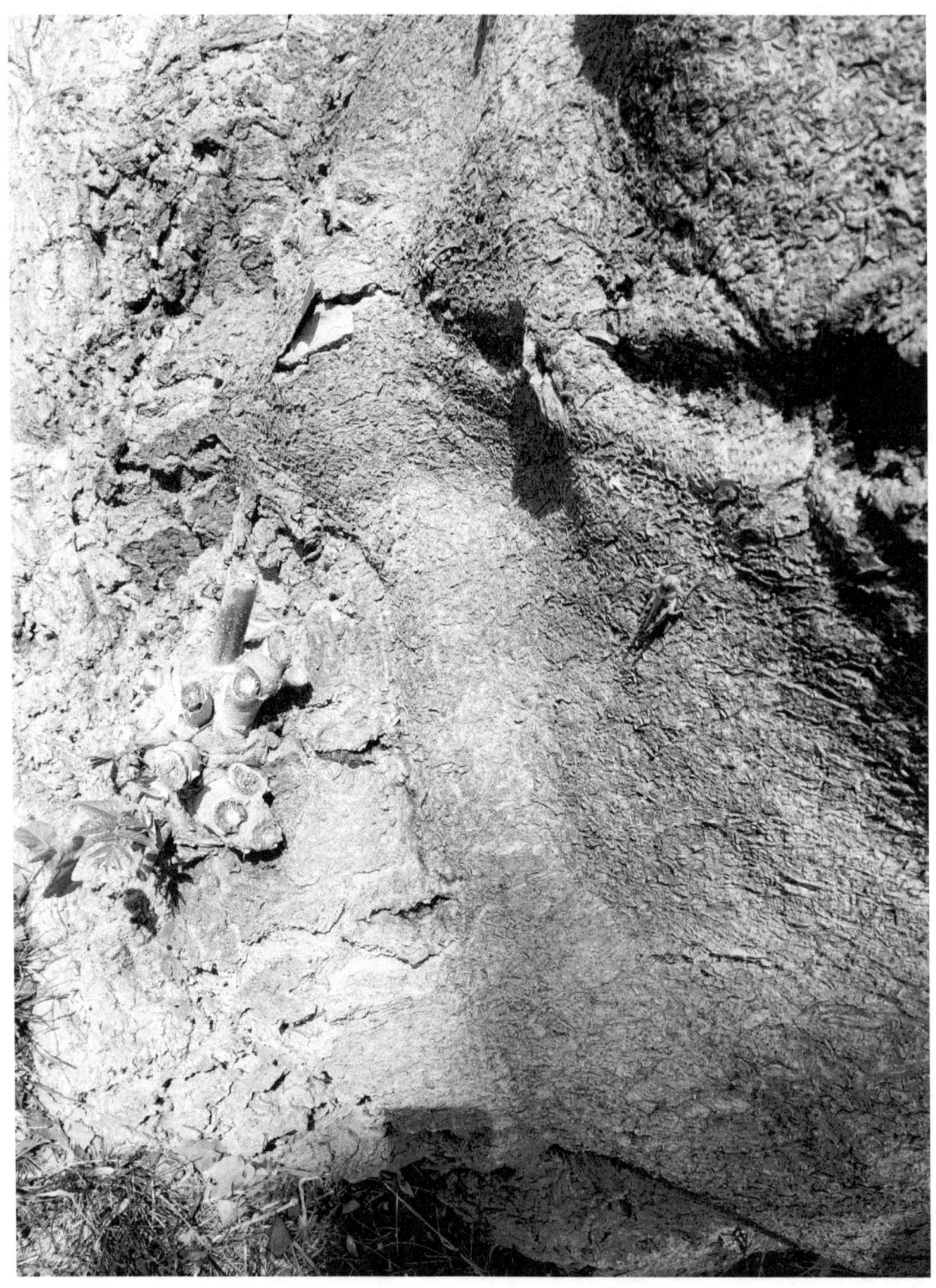

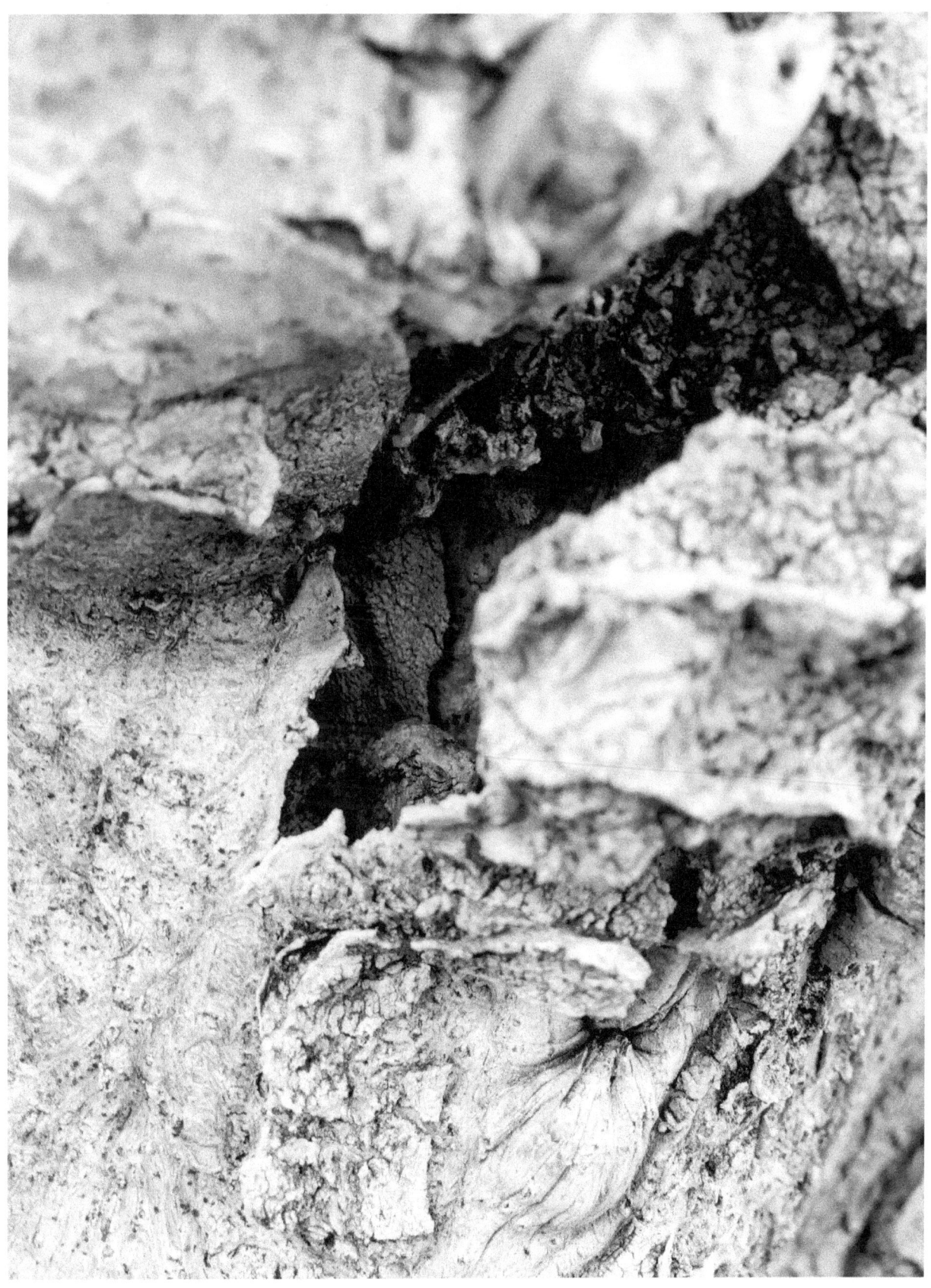

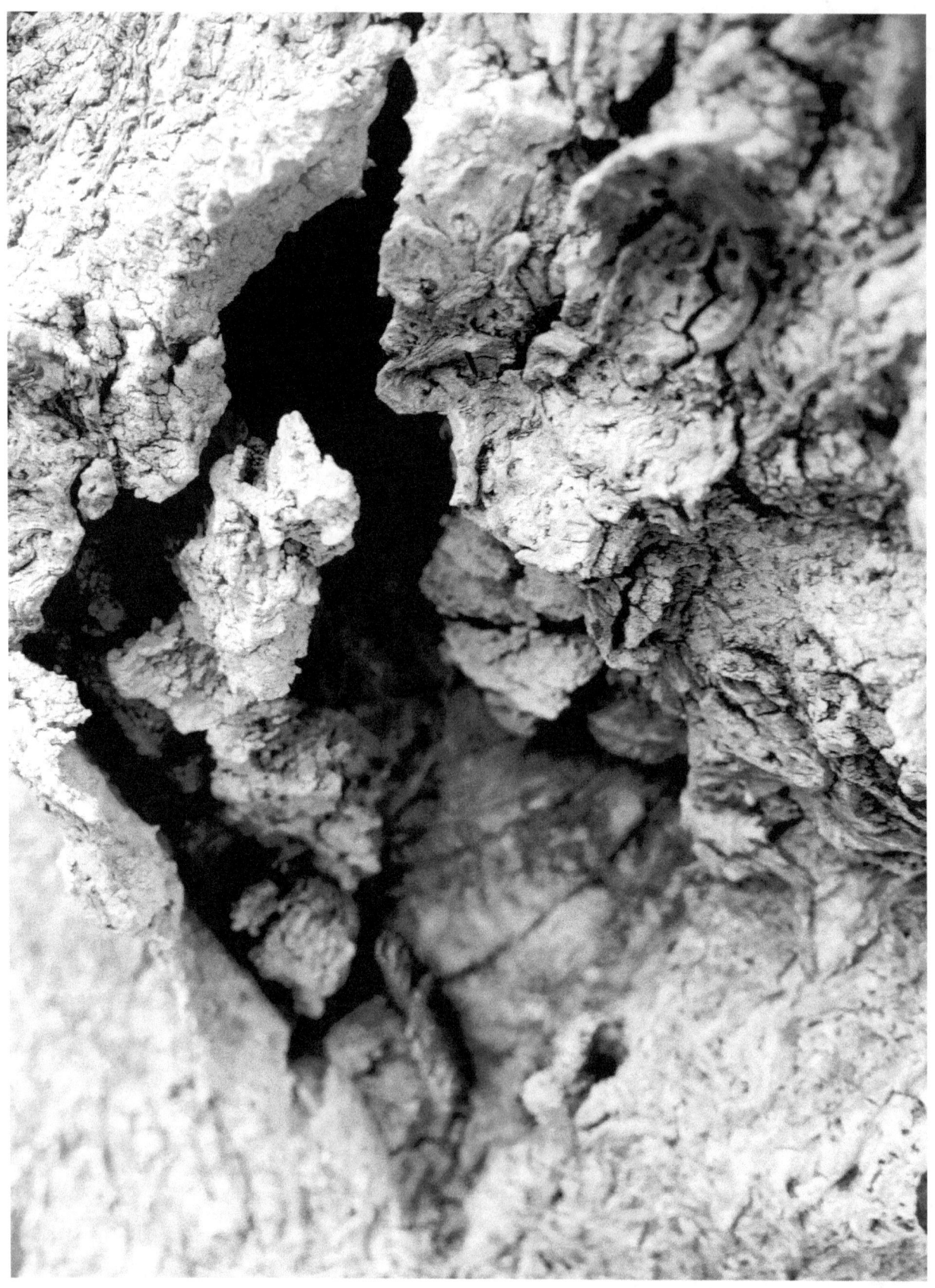

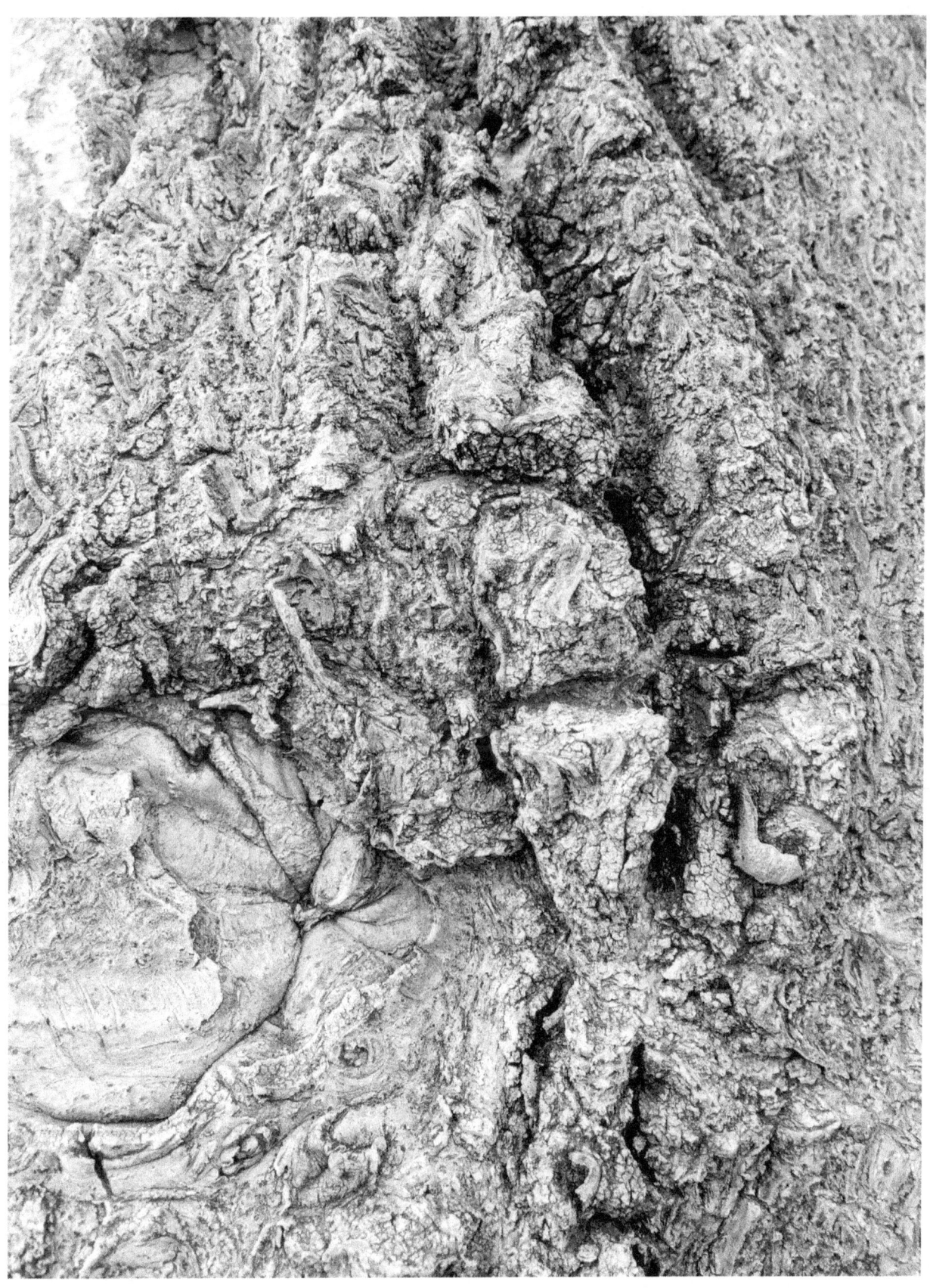

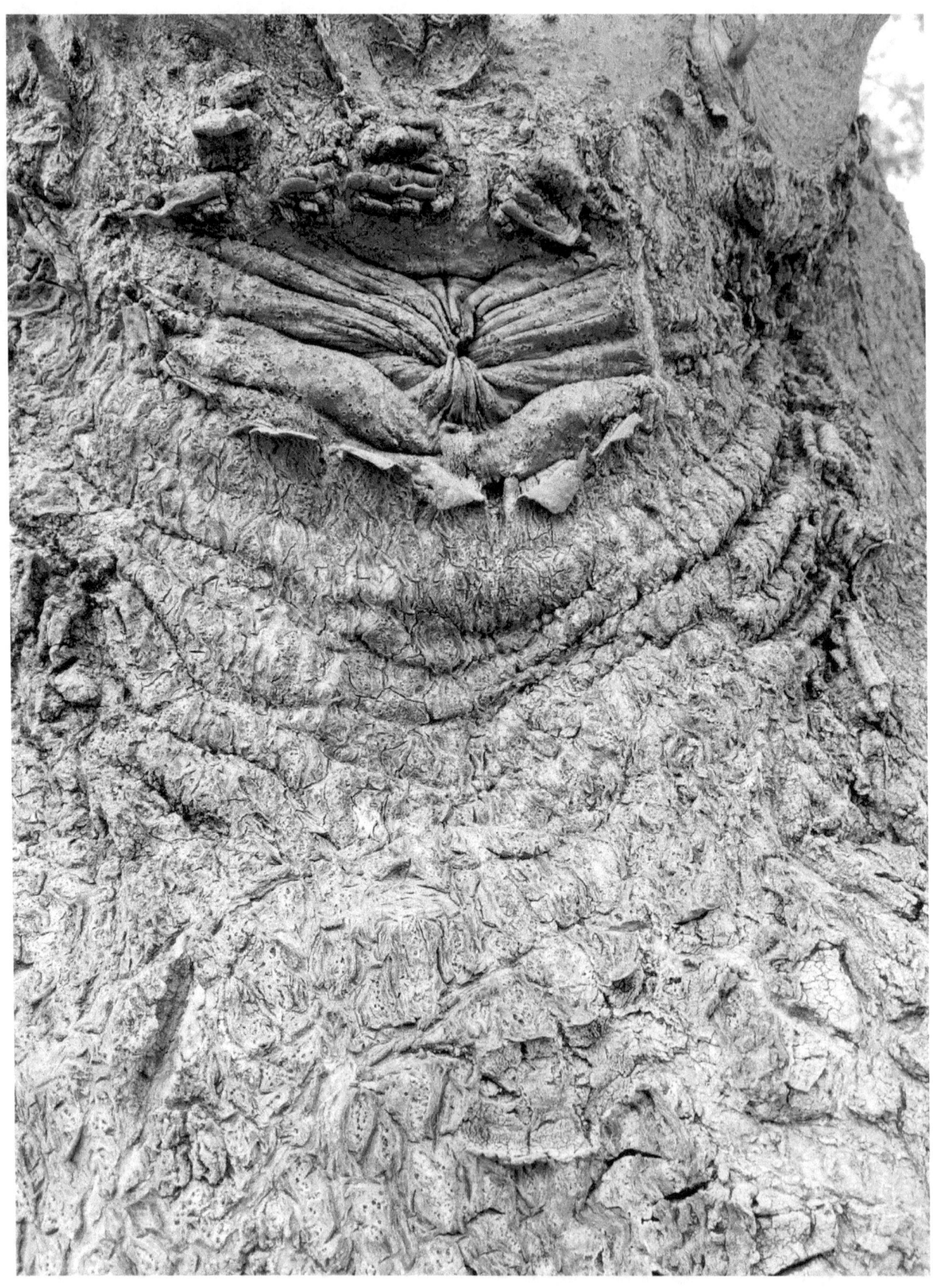

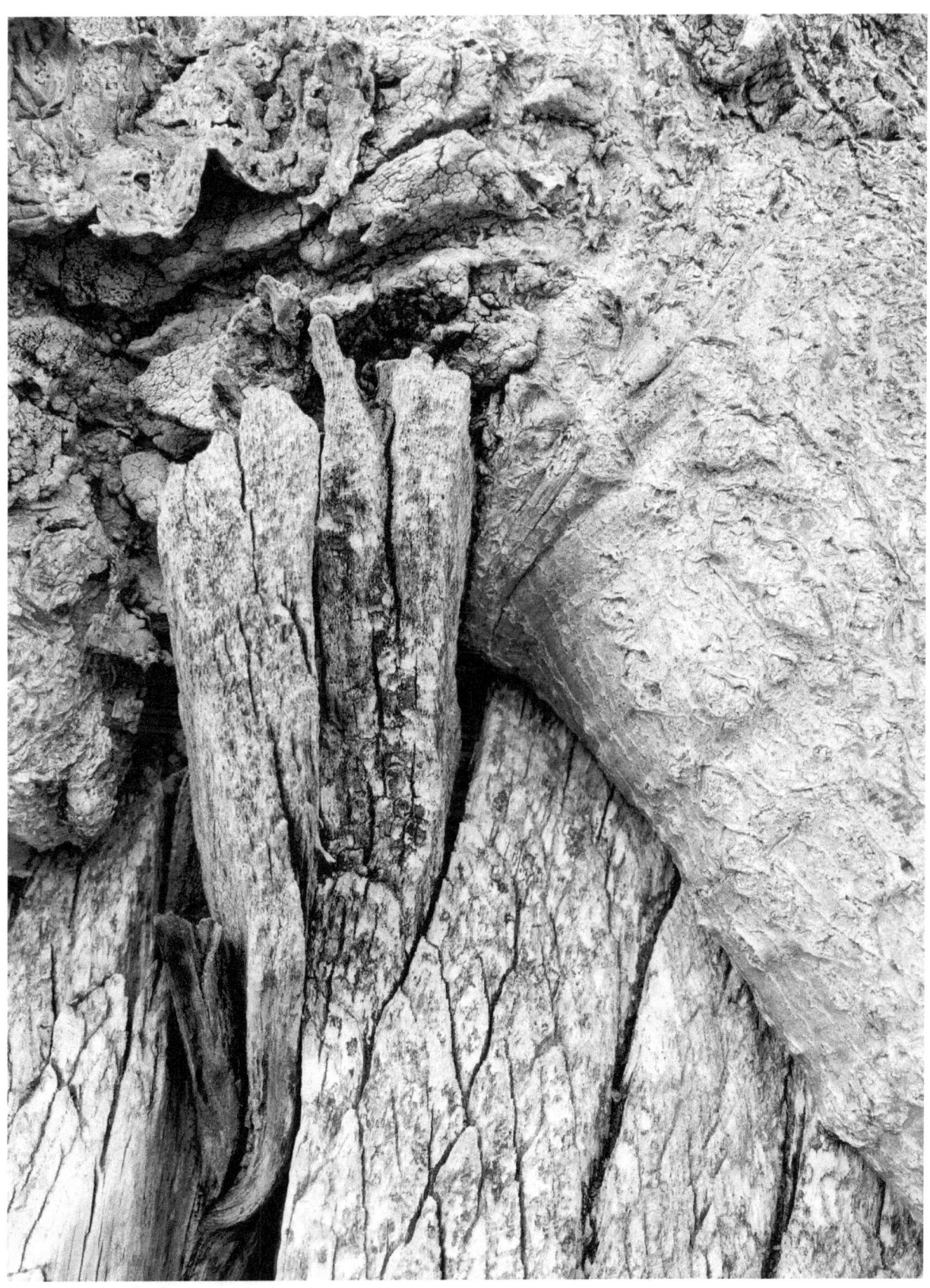

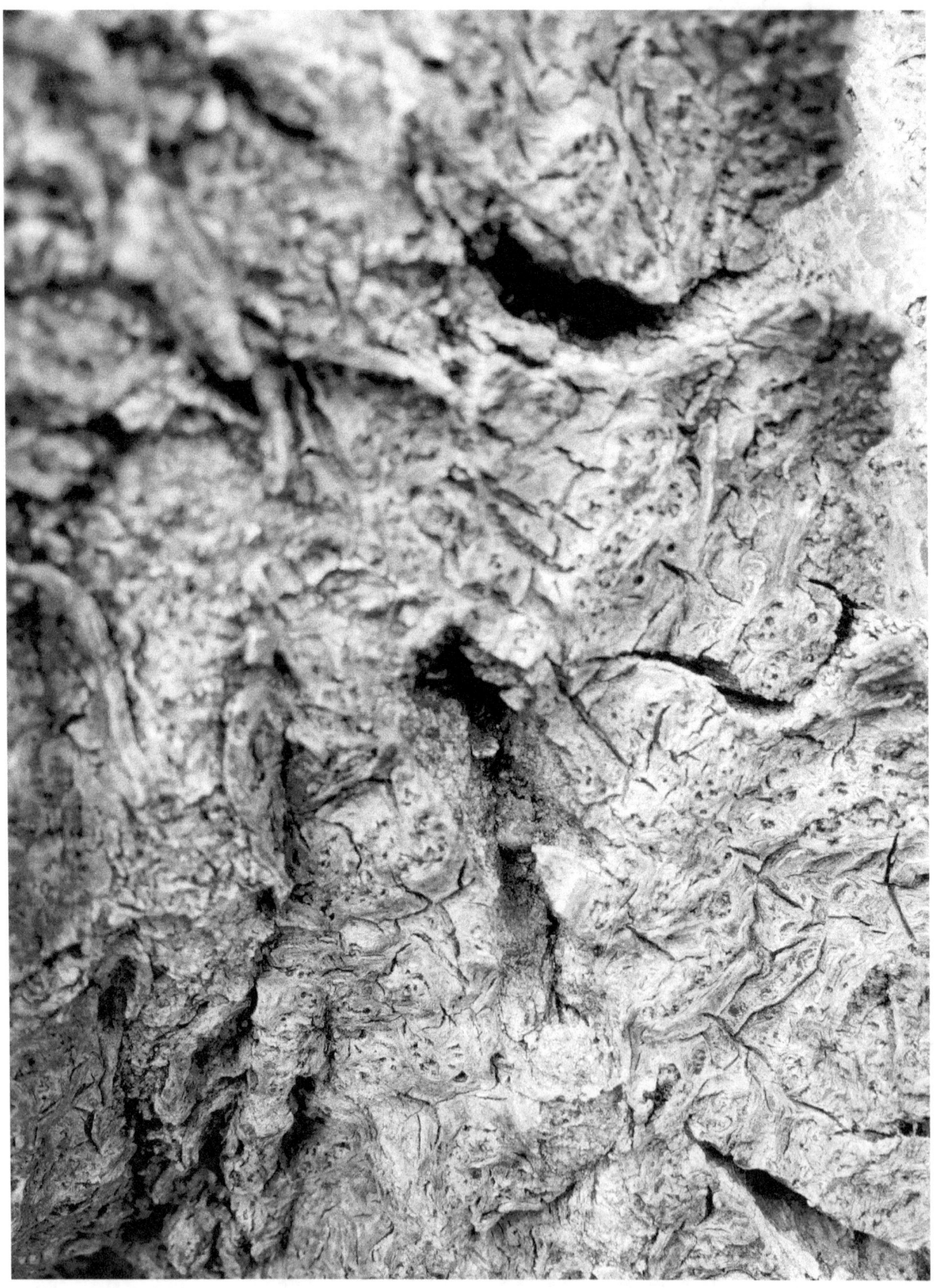

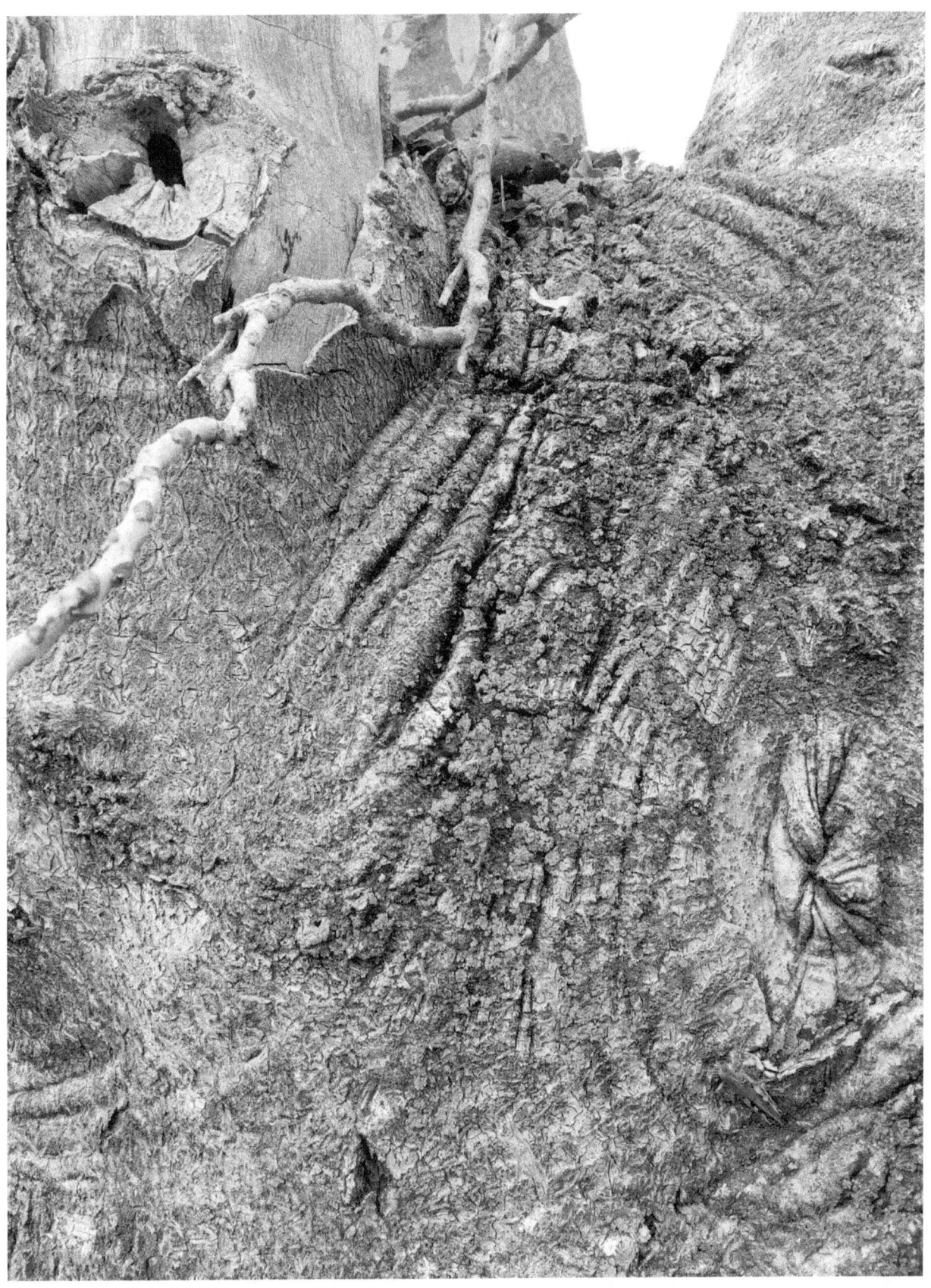

27

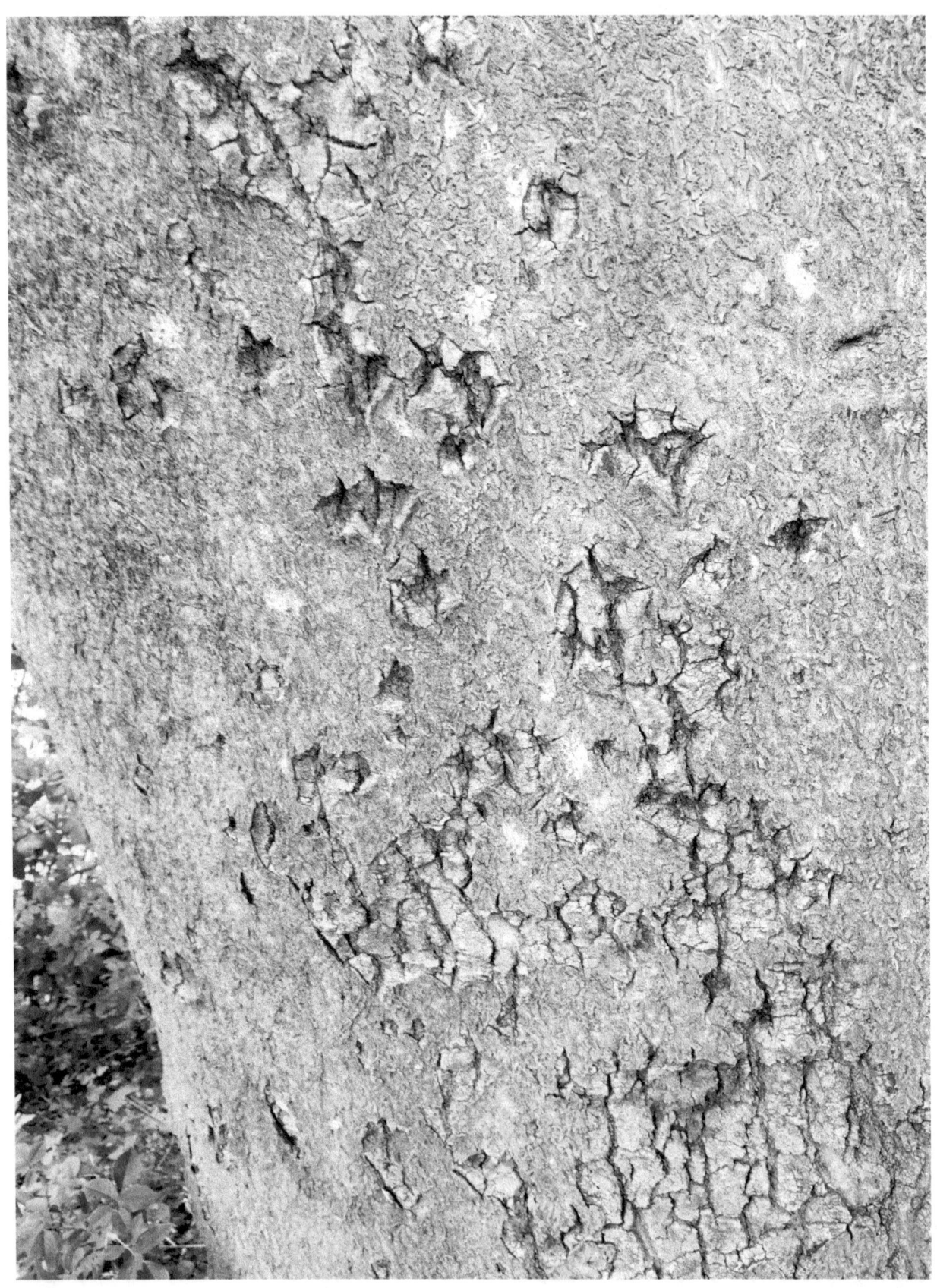

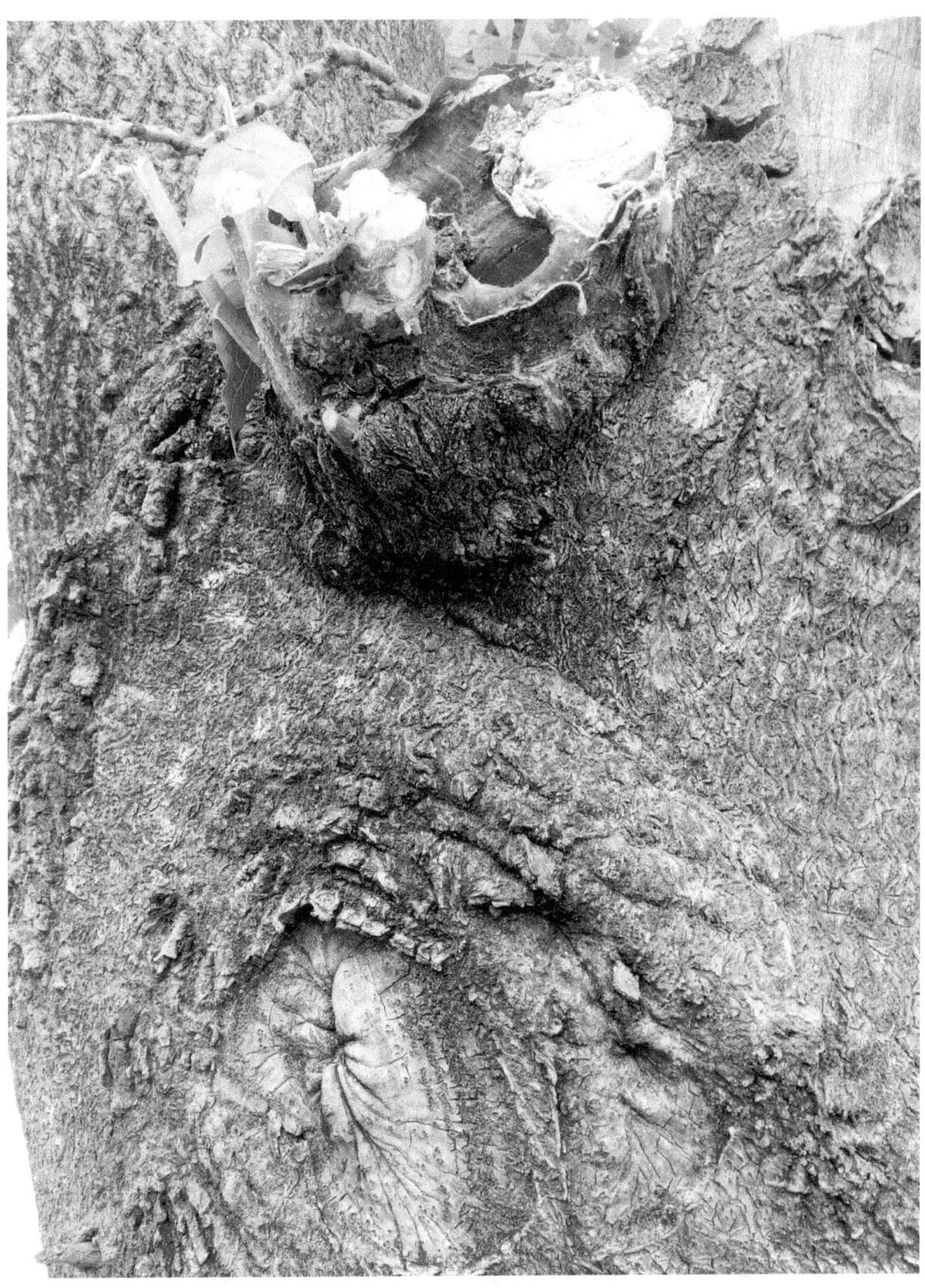

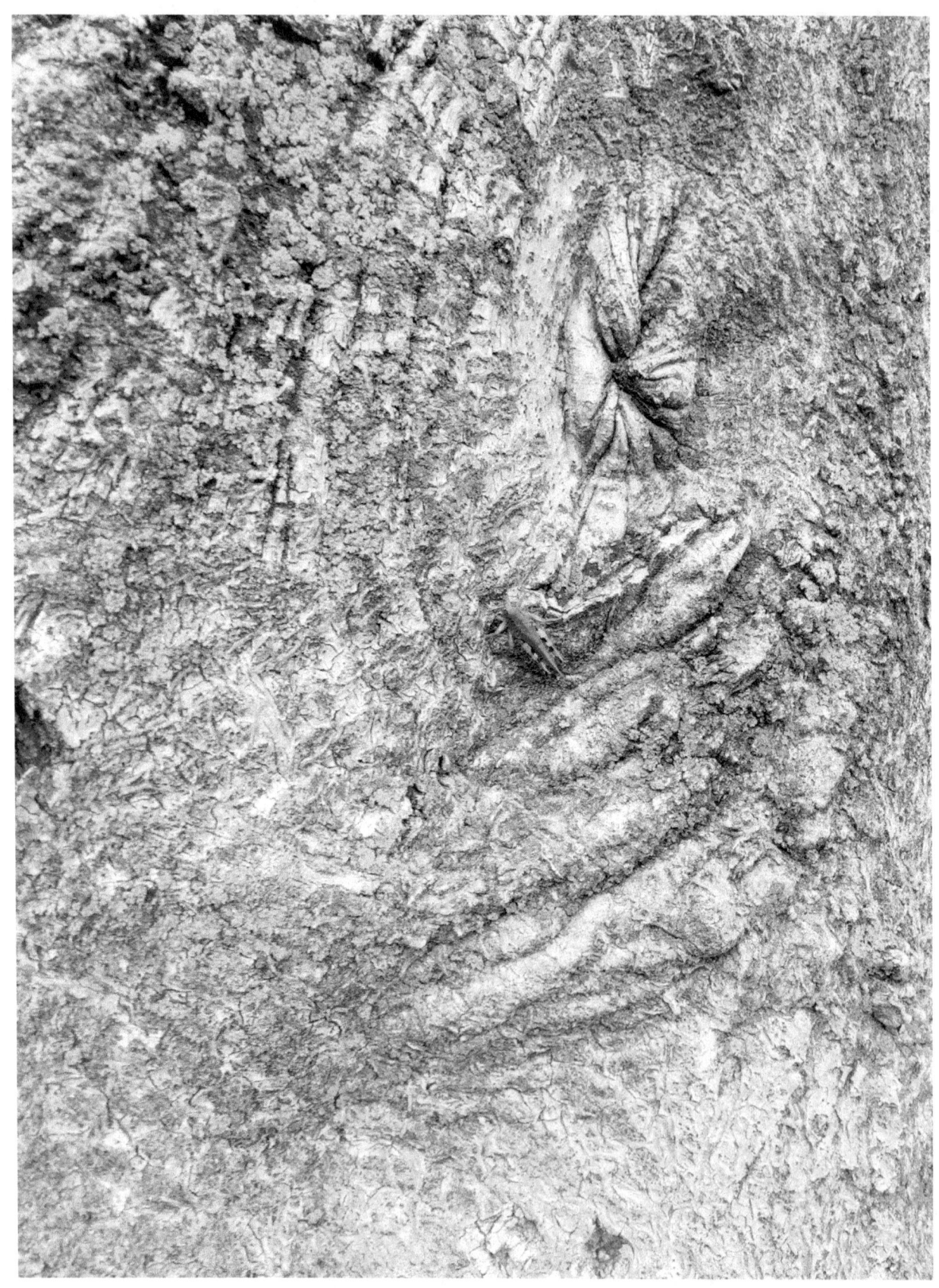

30

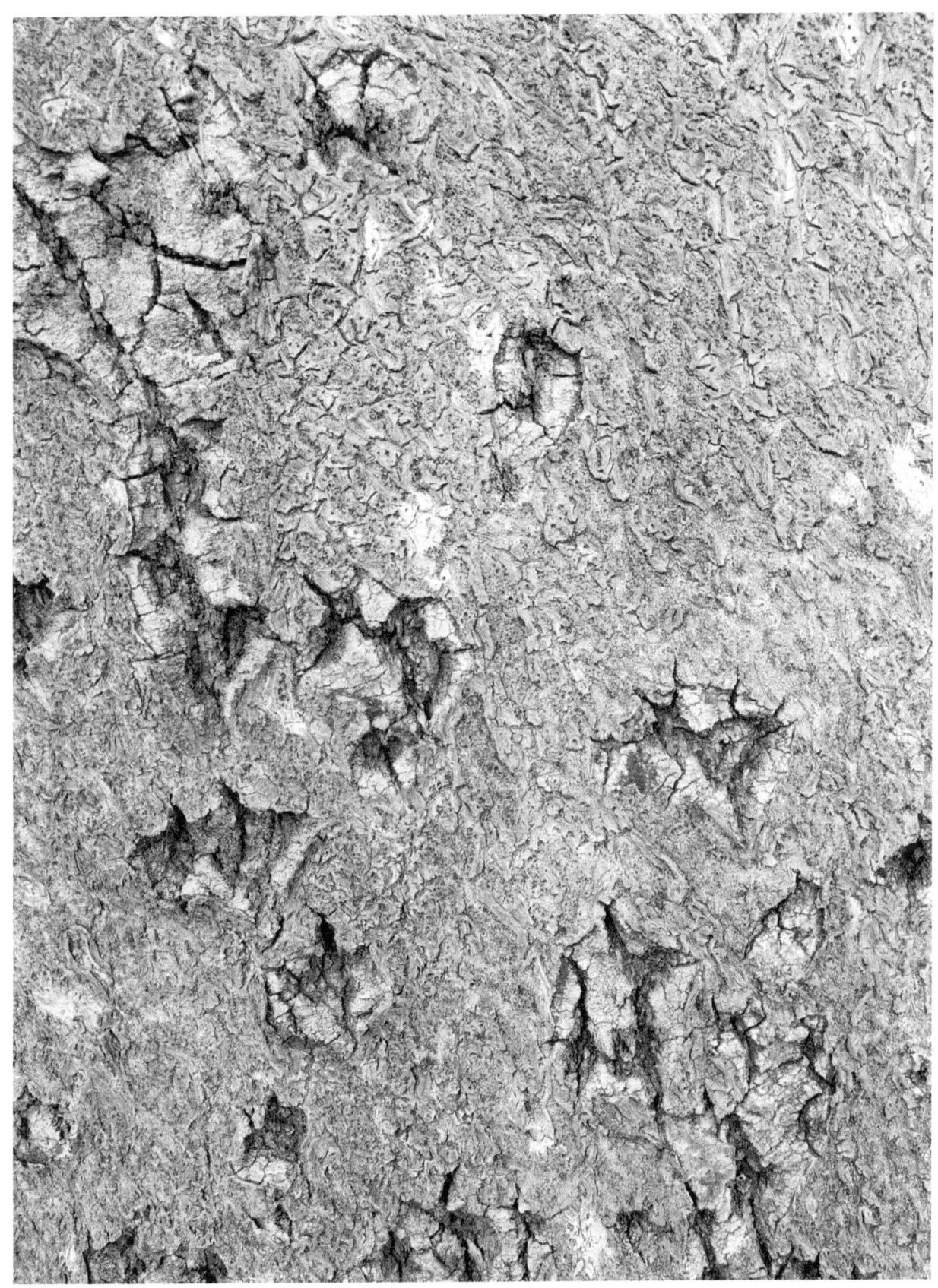

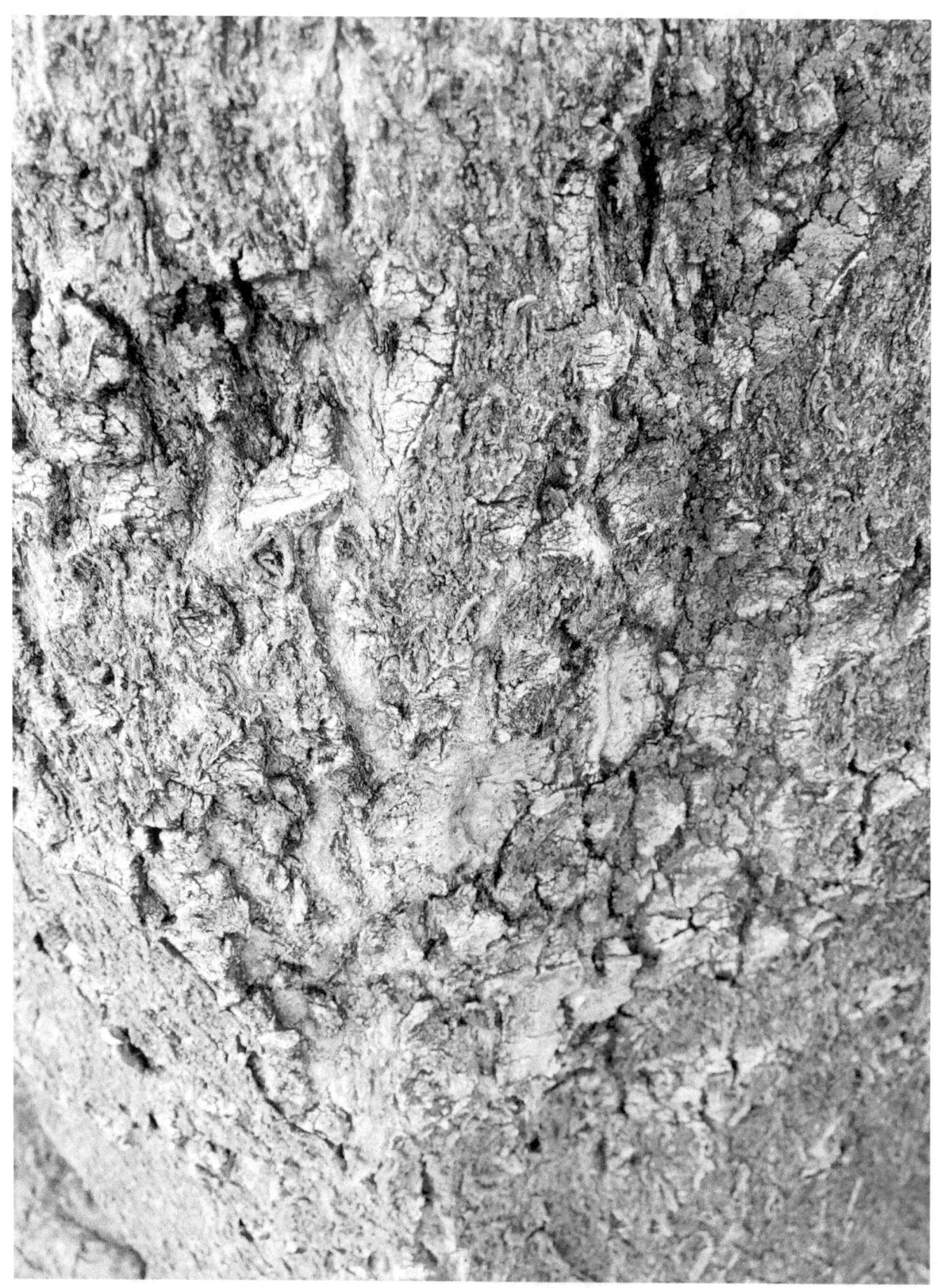

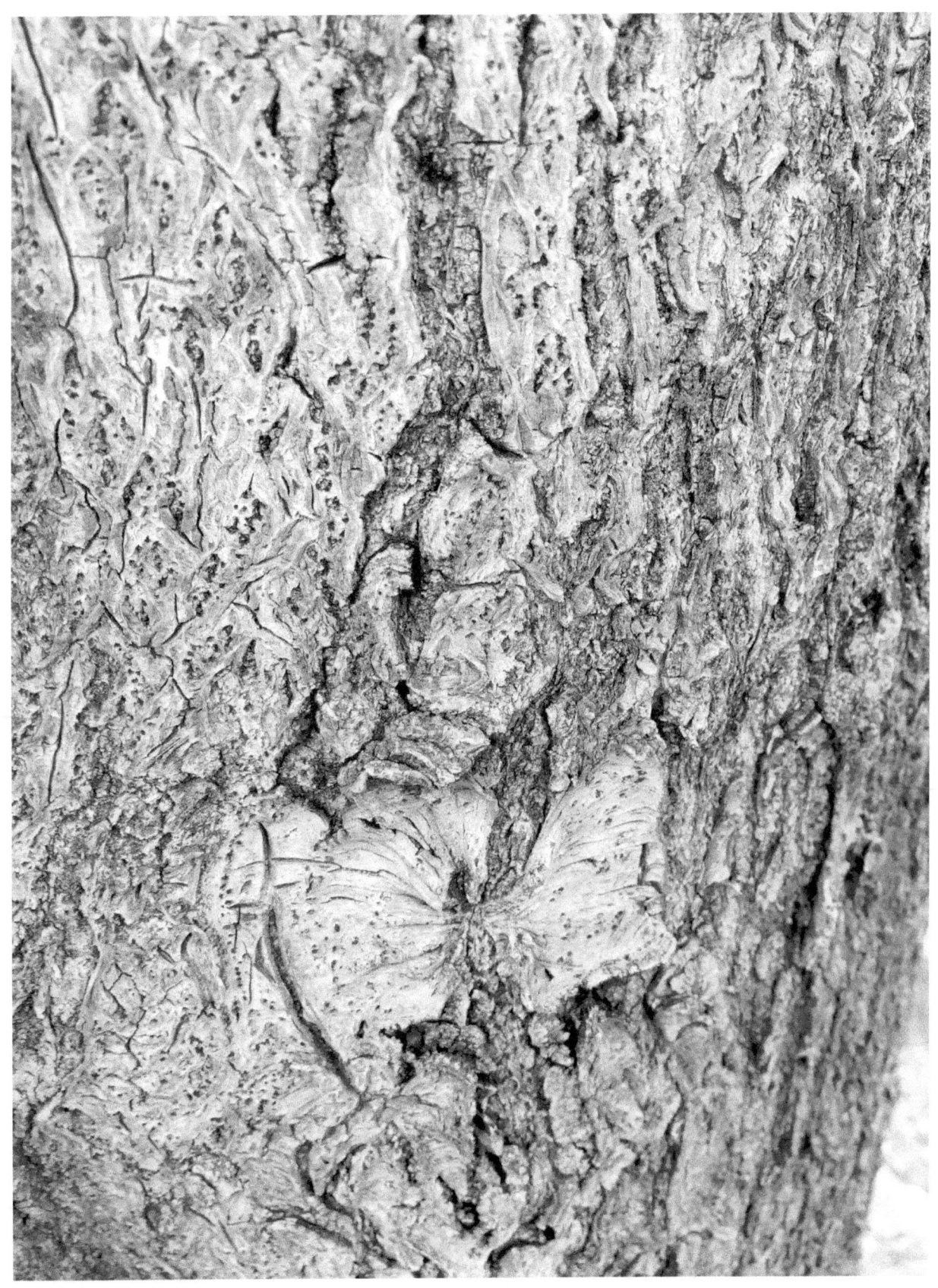

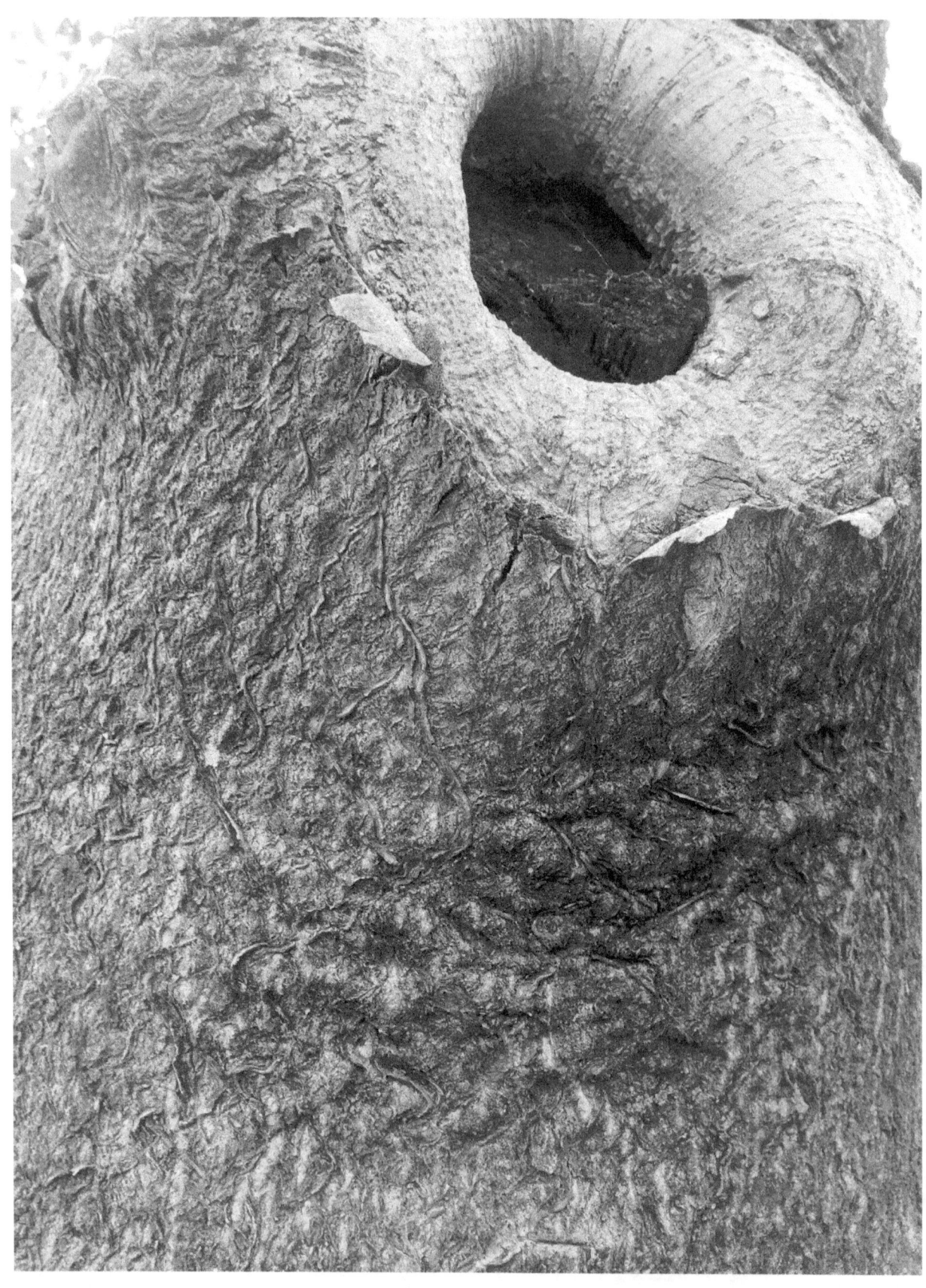

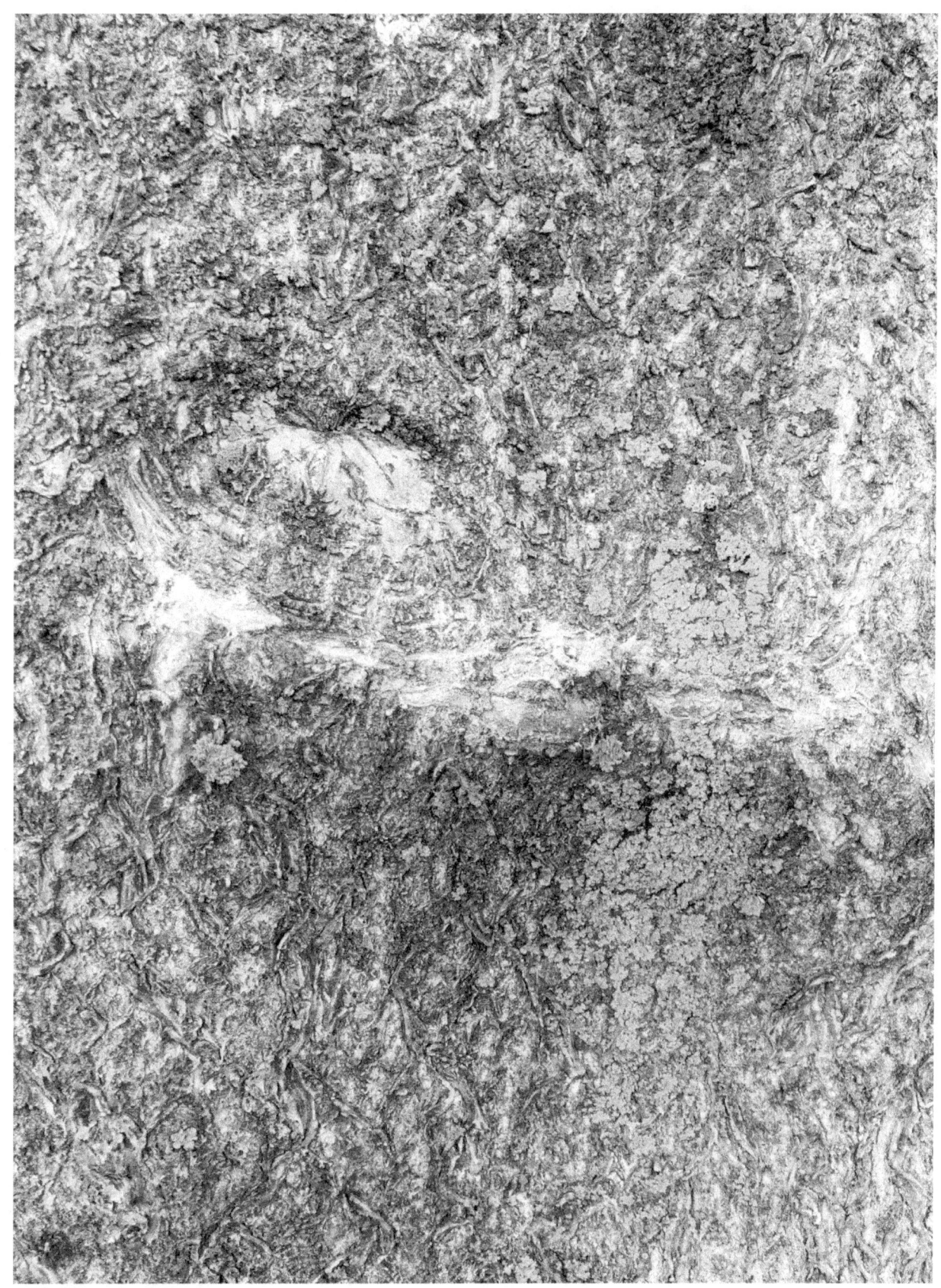

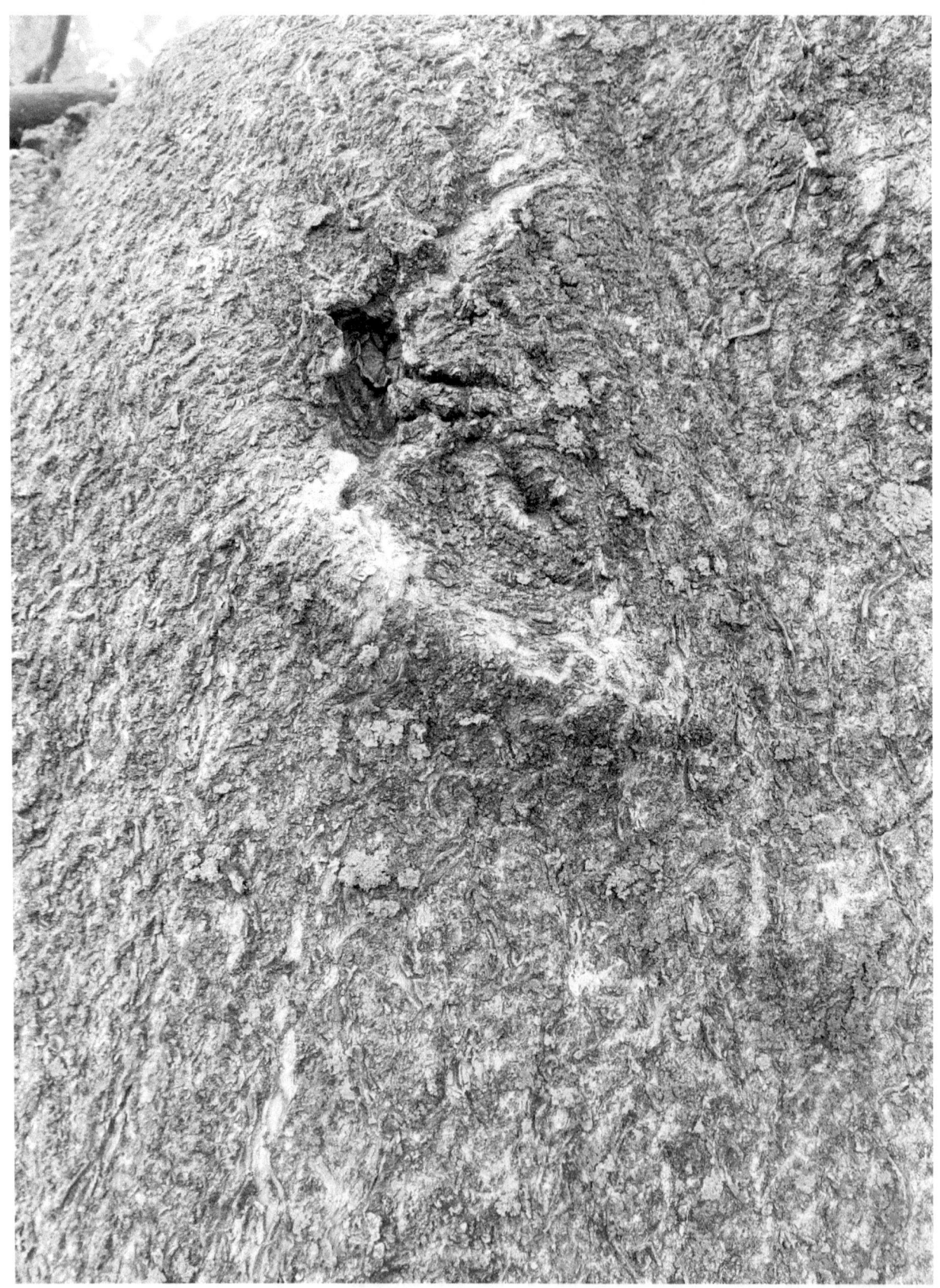

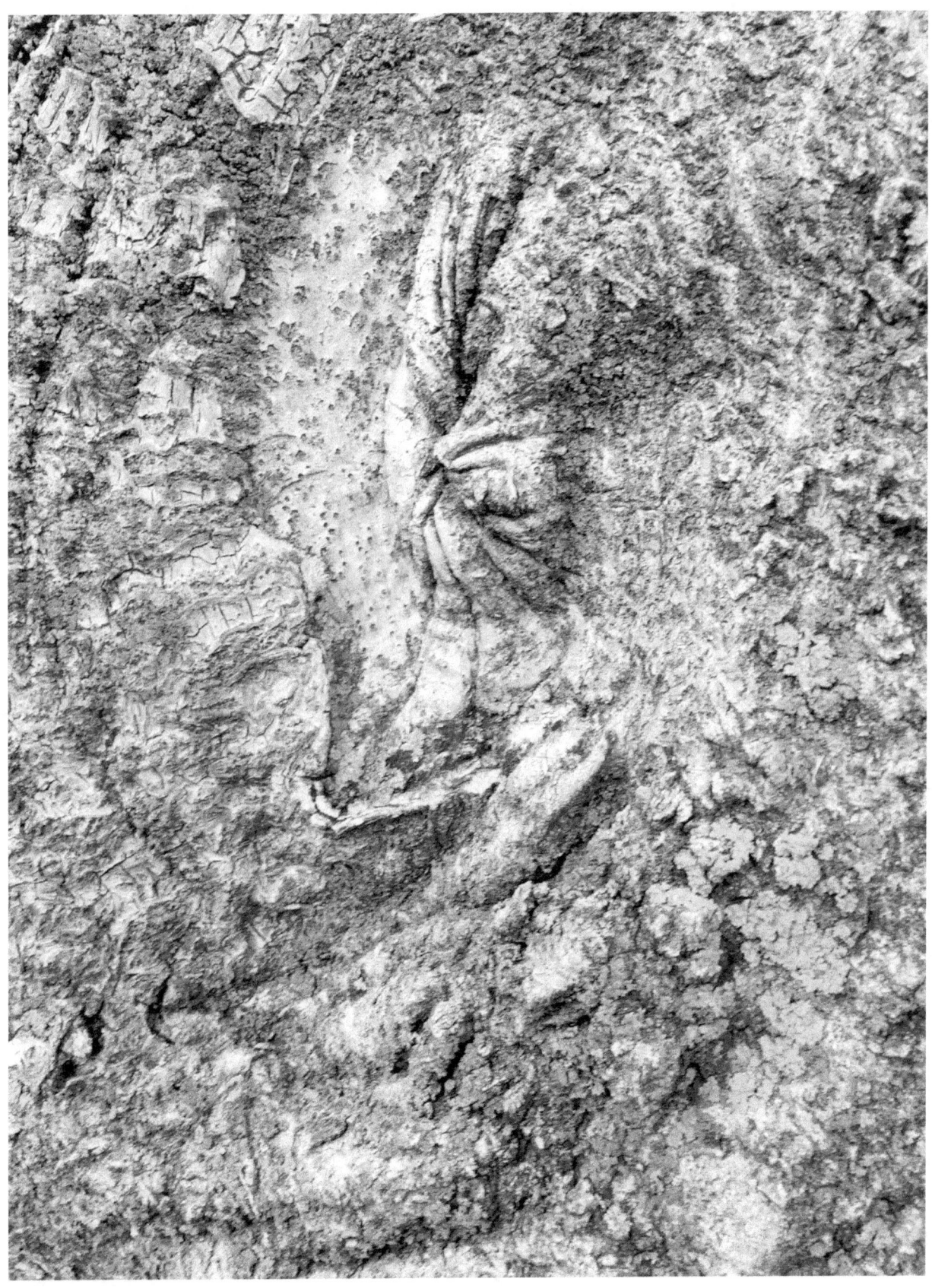

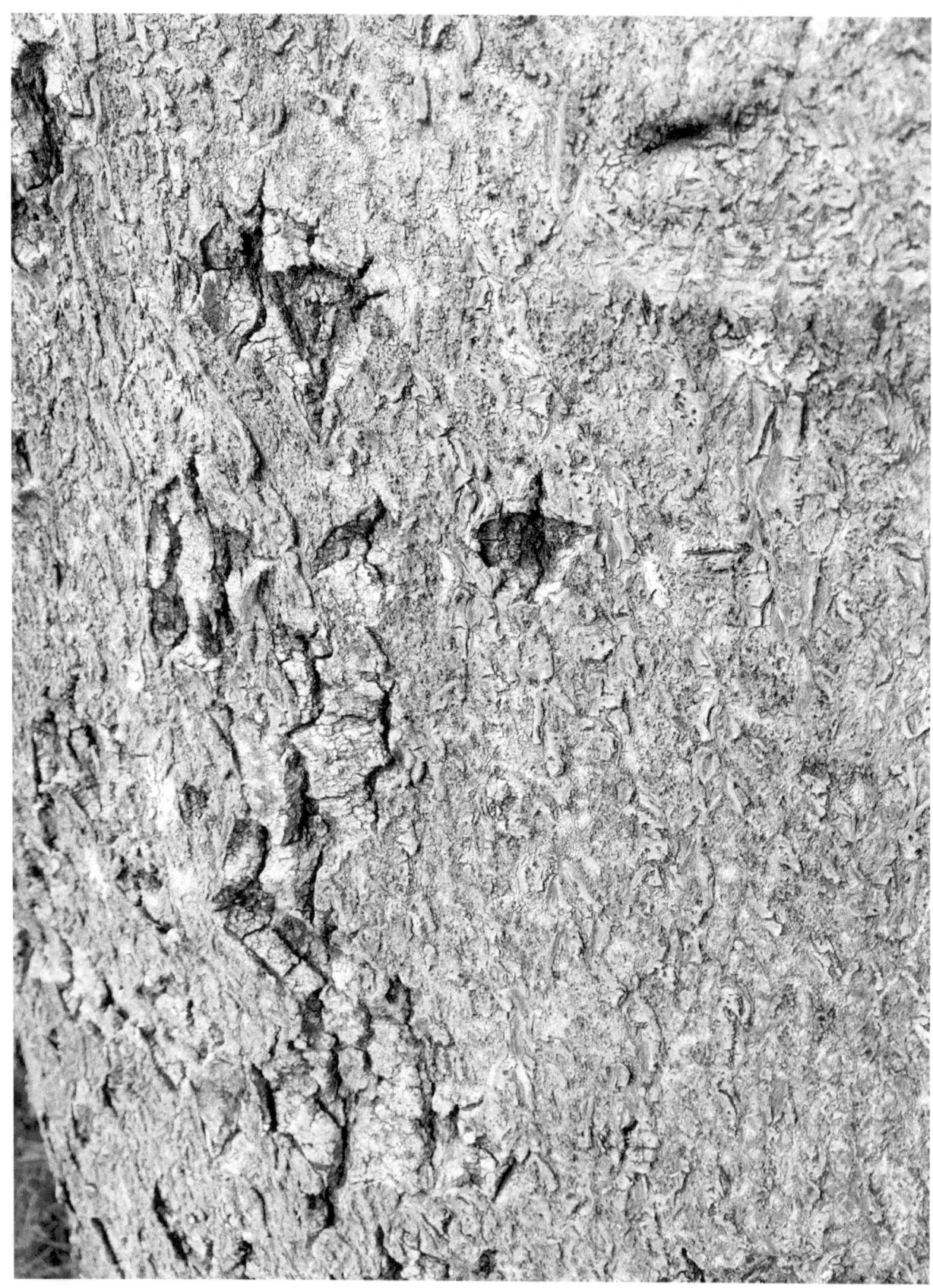

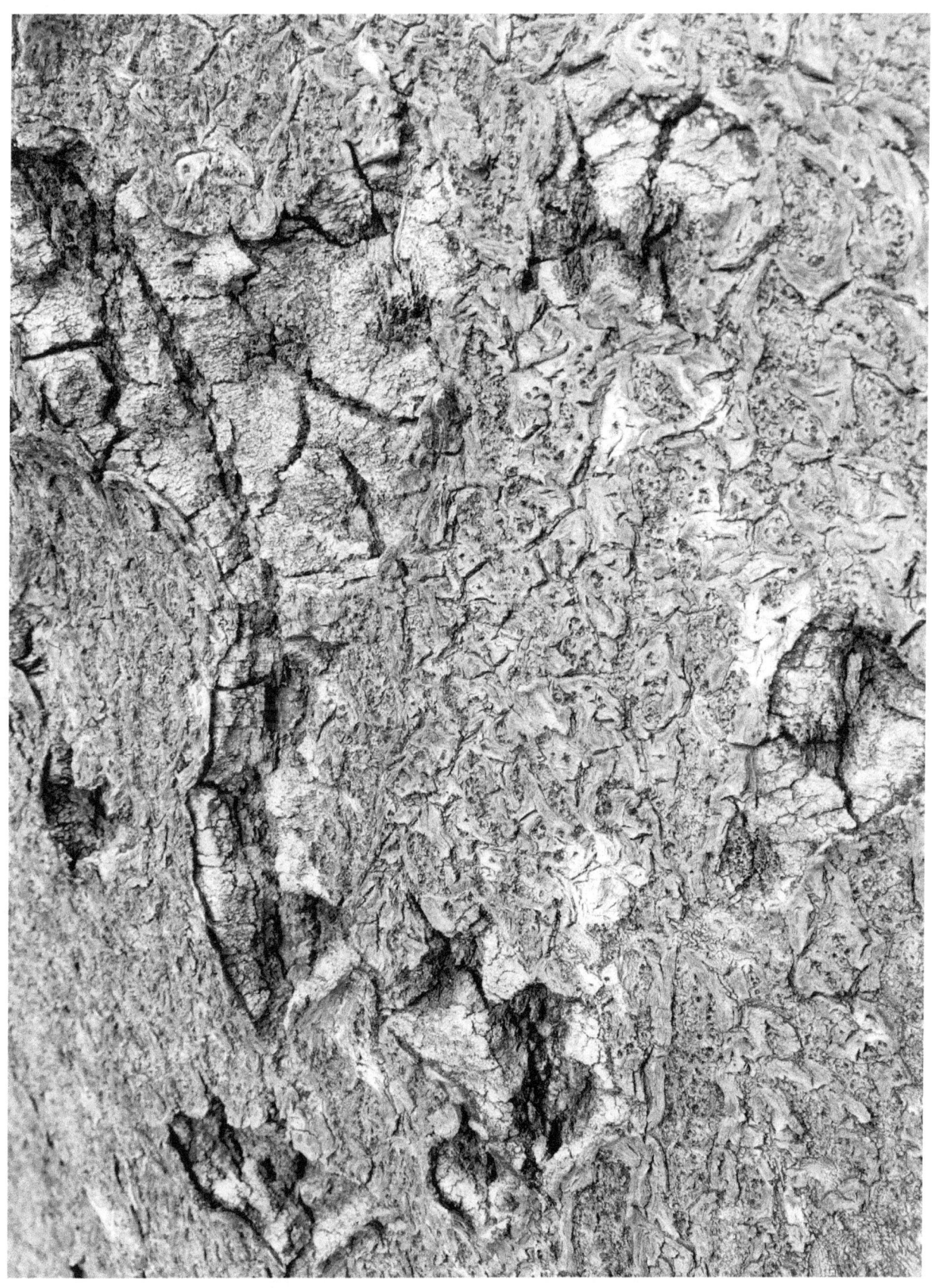

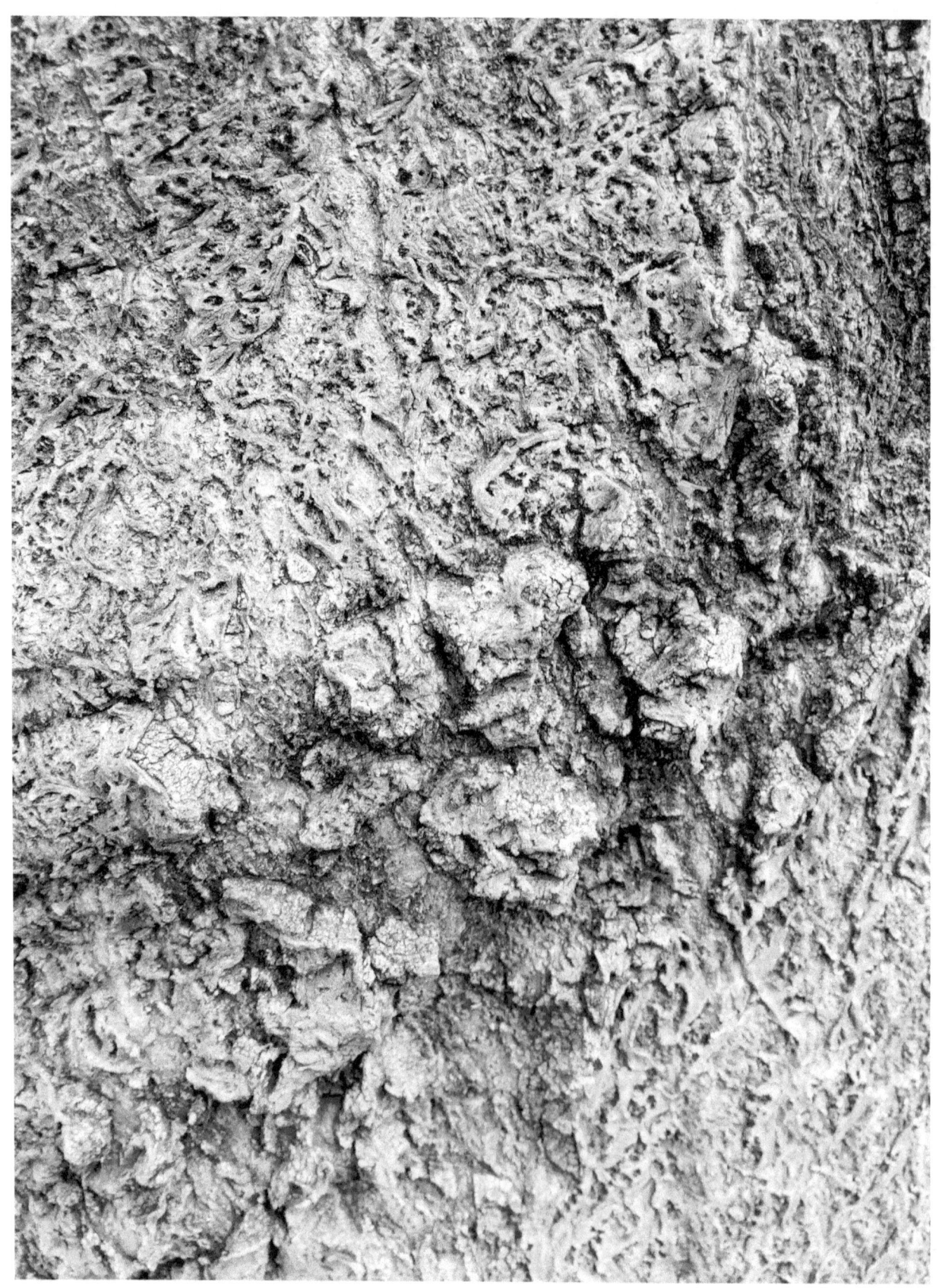

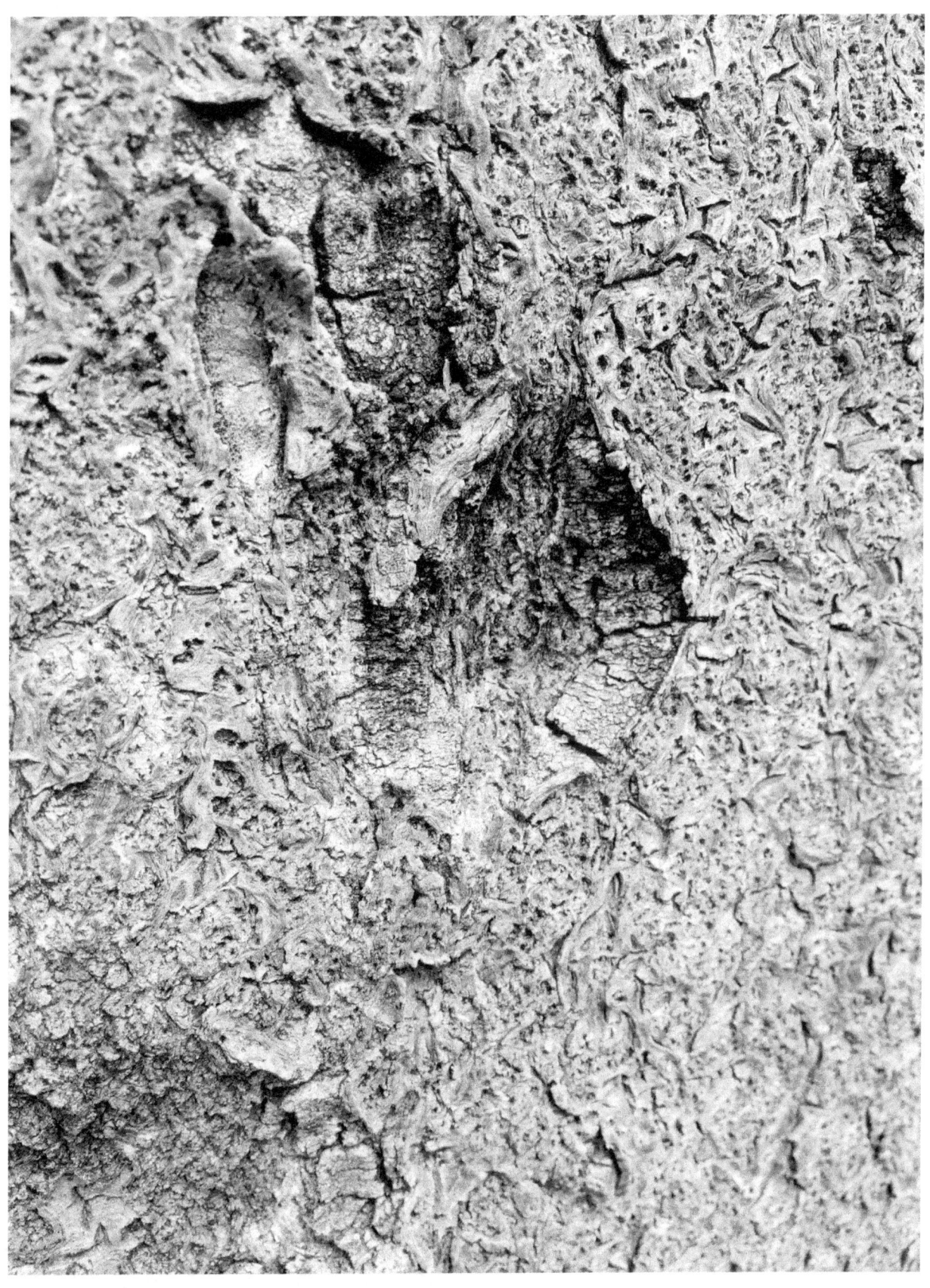

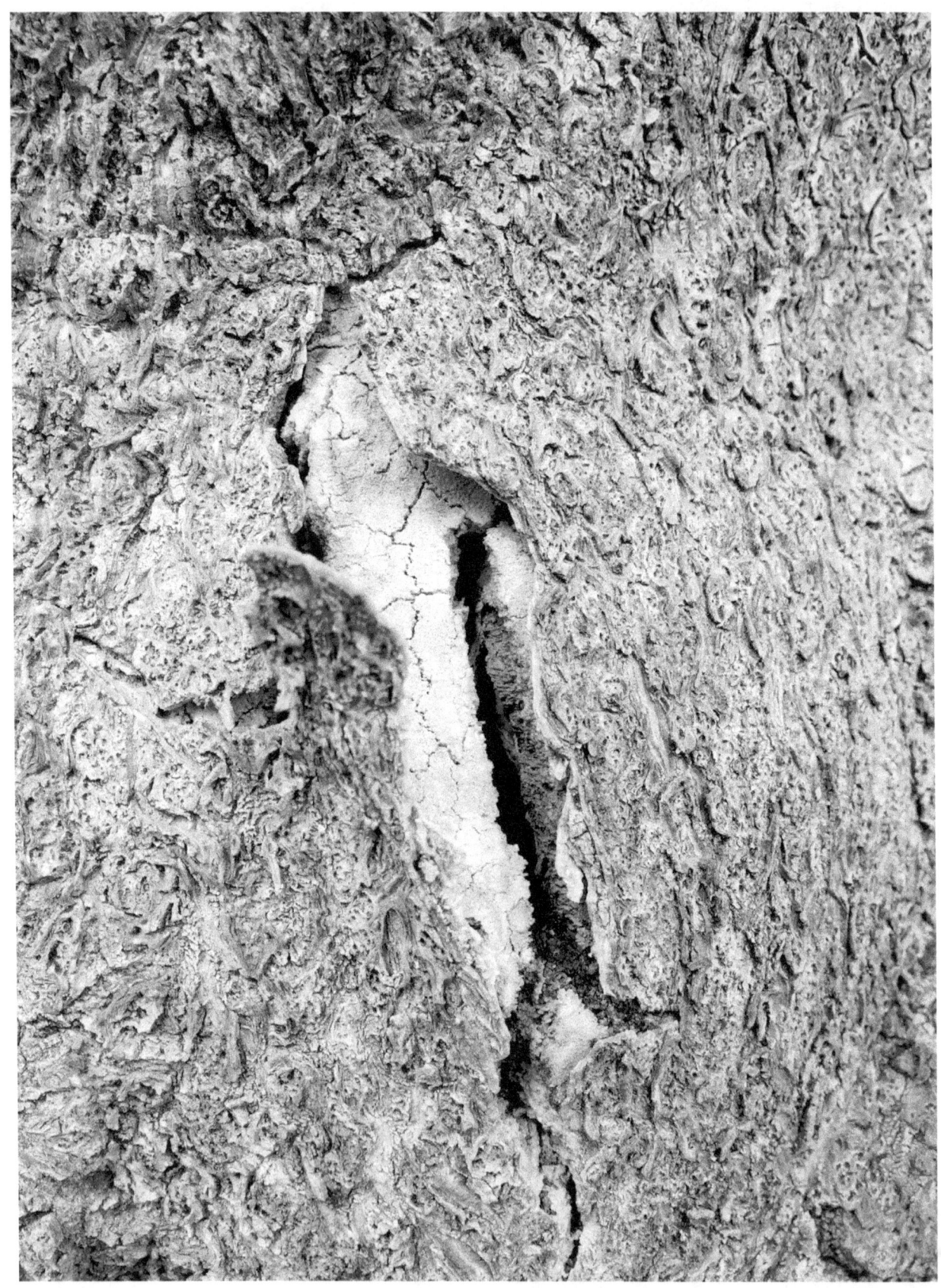

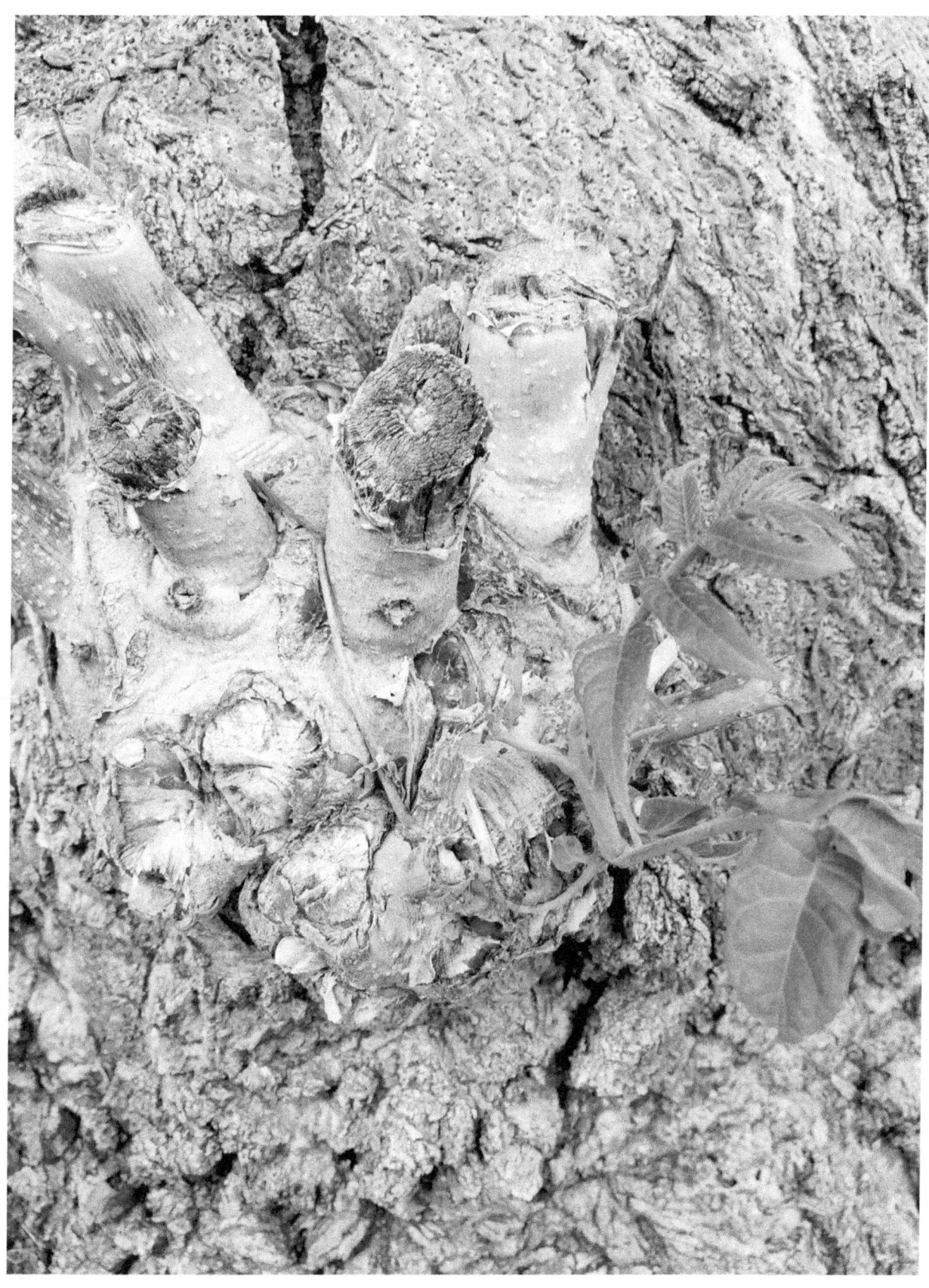

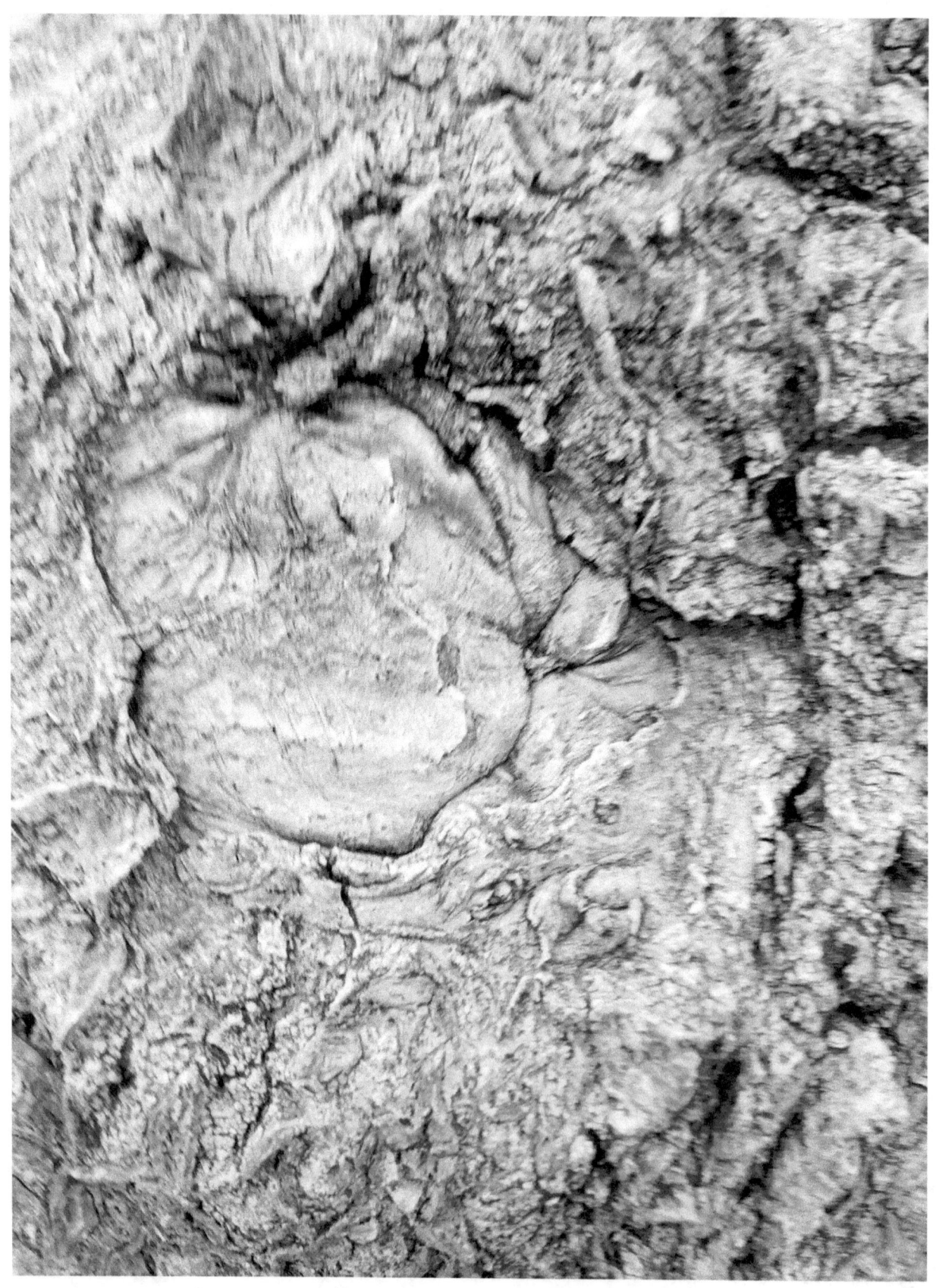

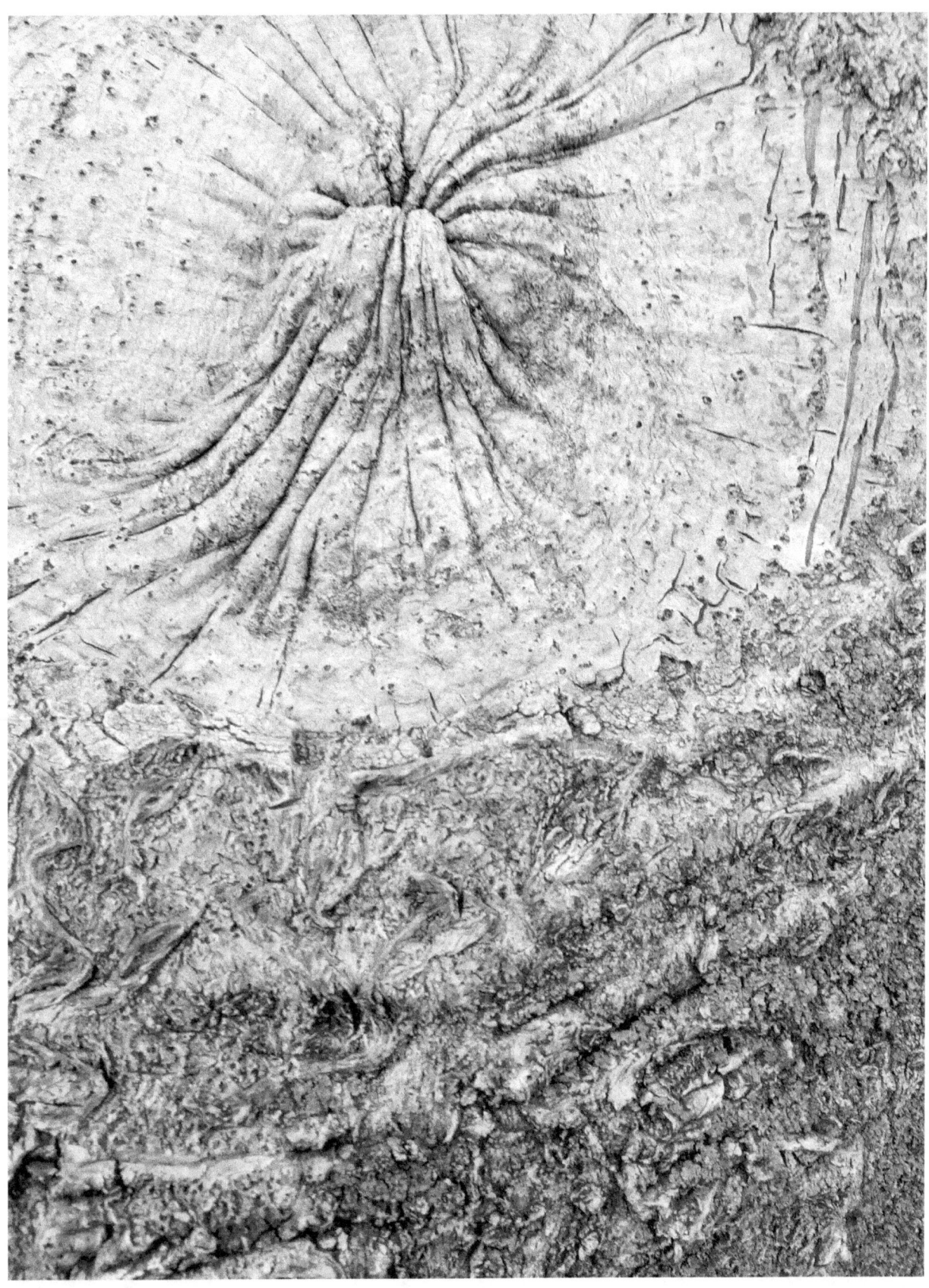

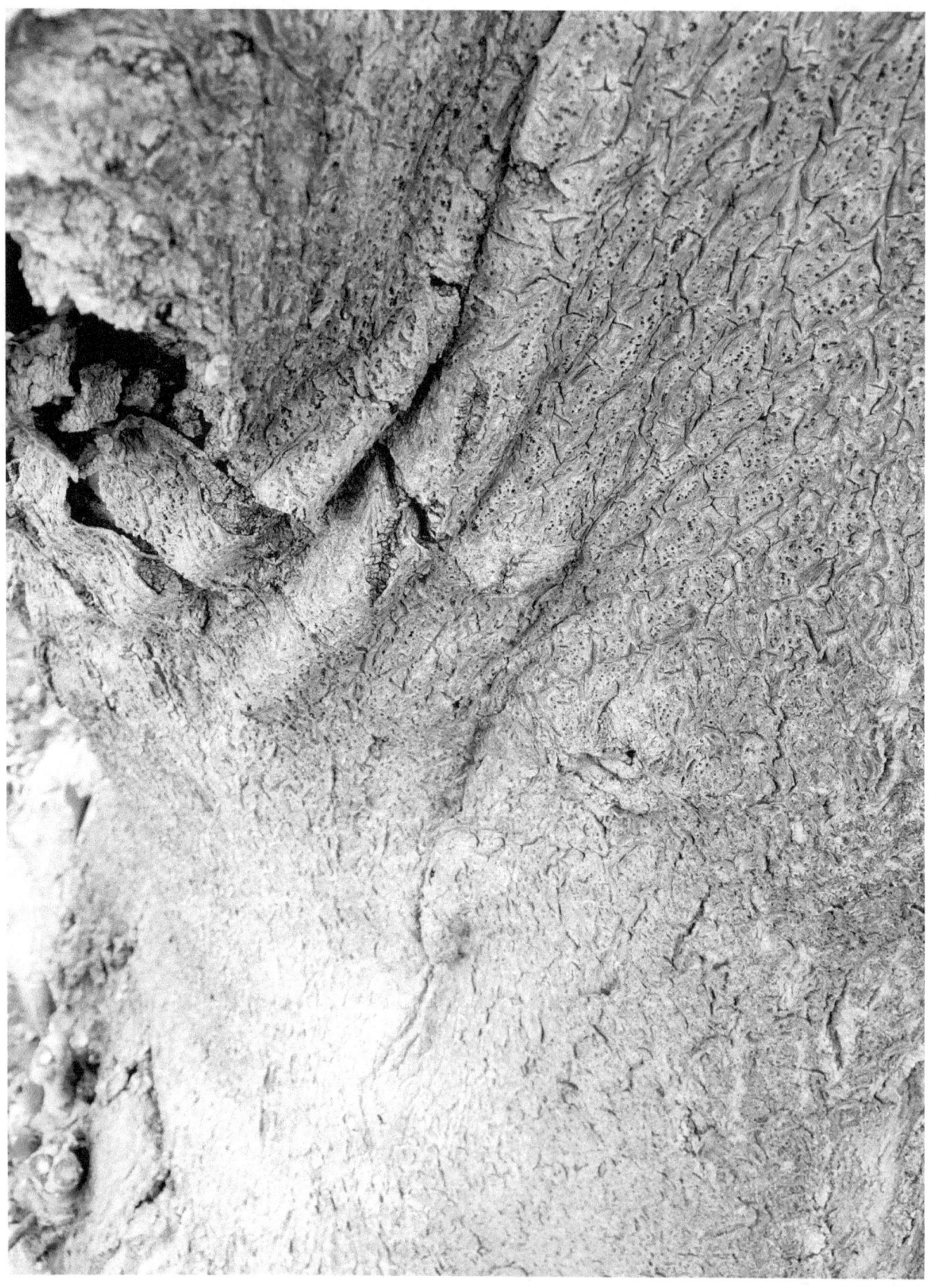

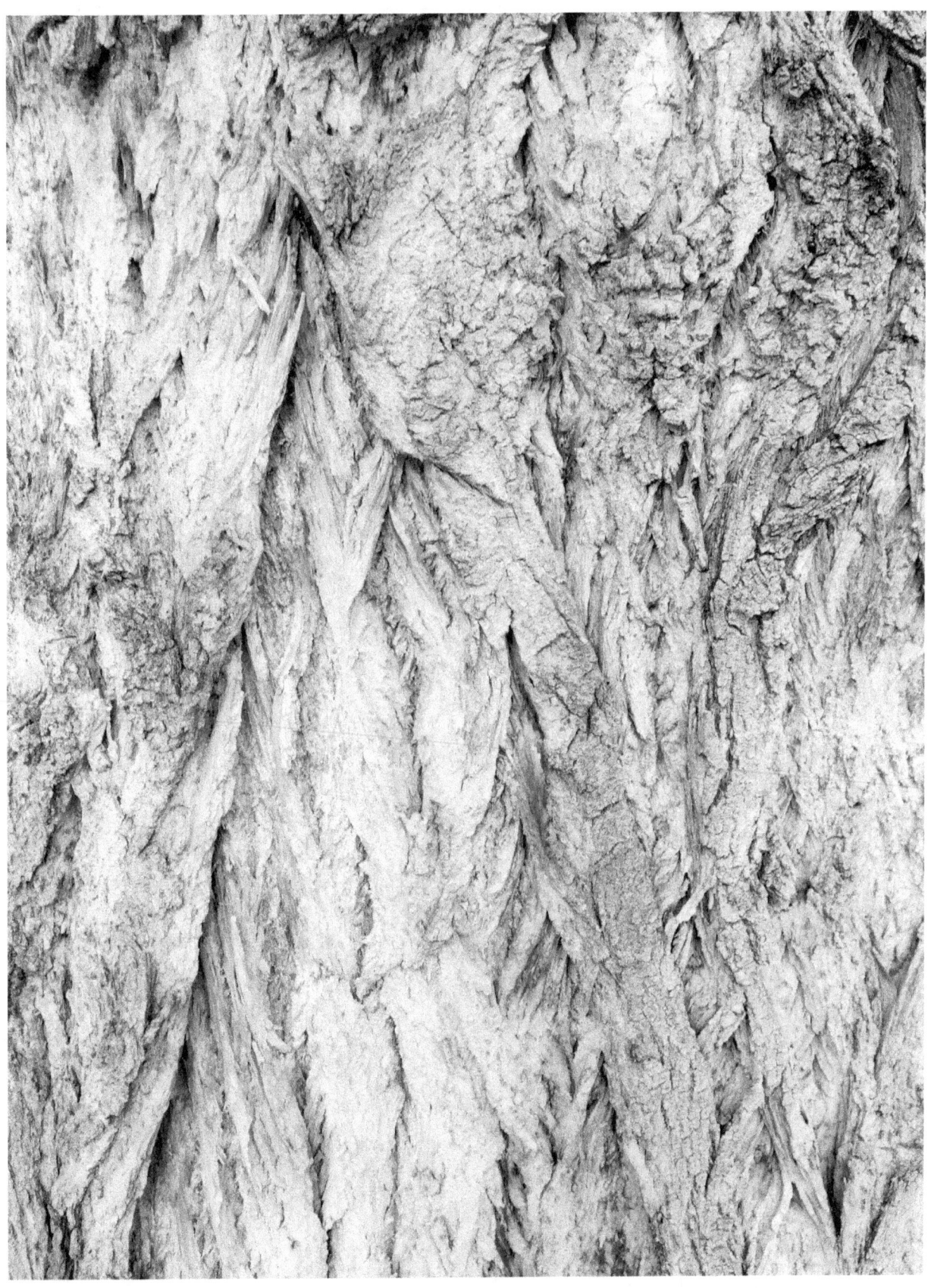

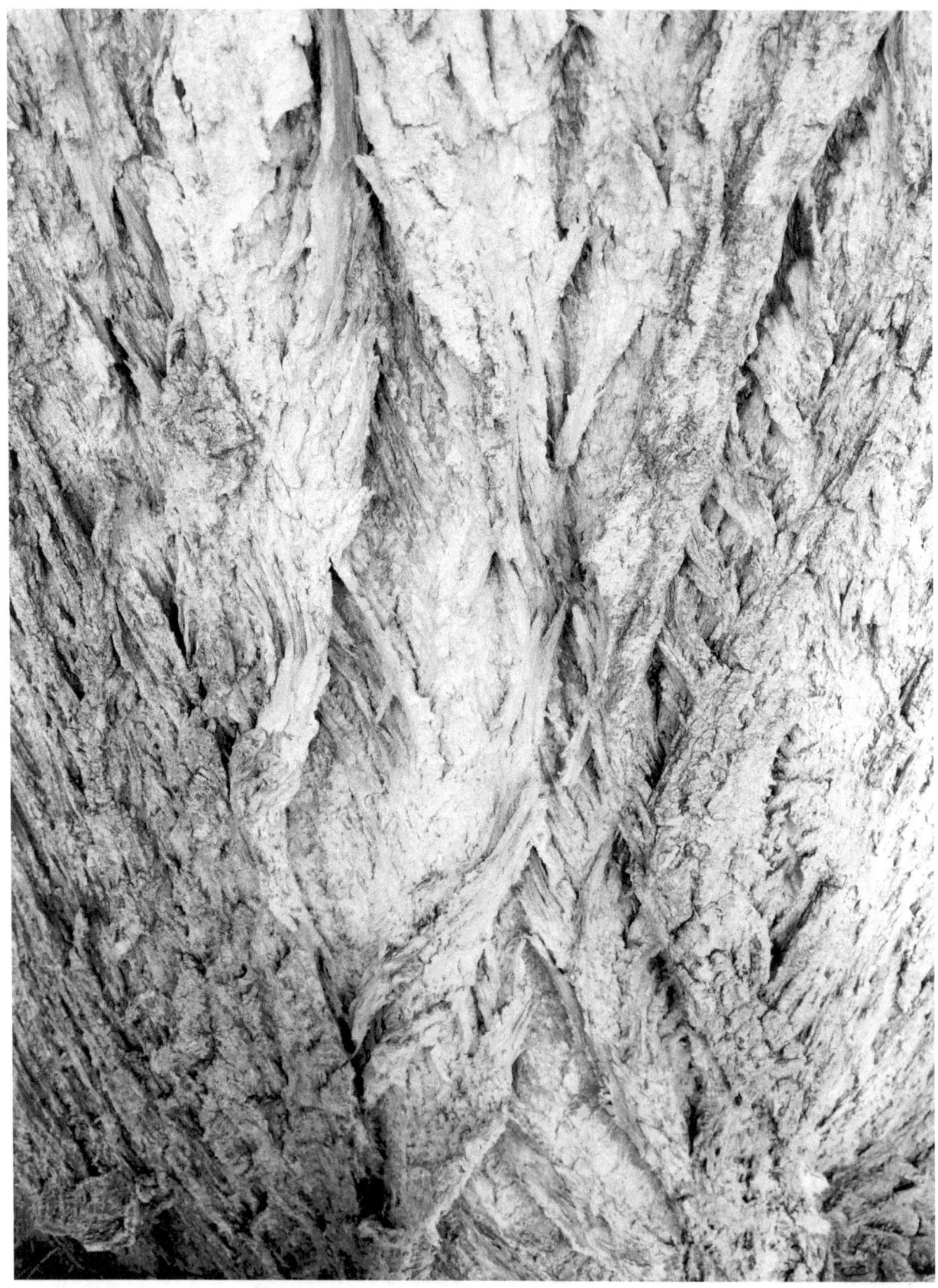

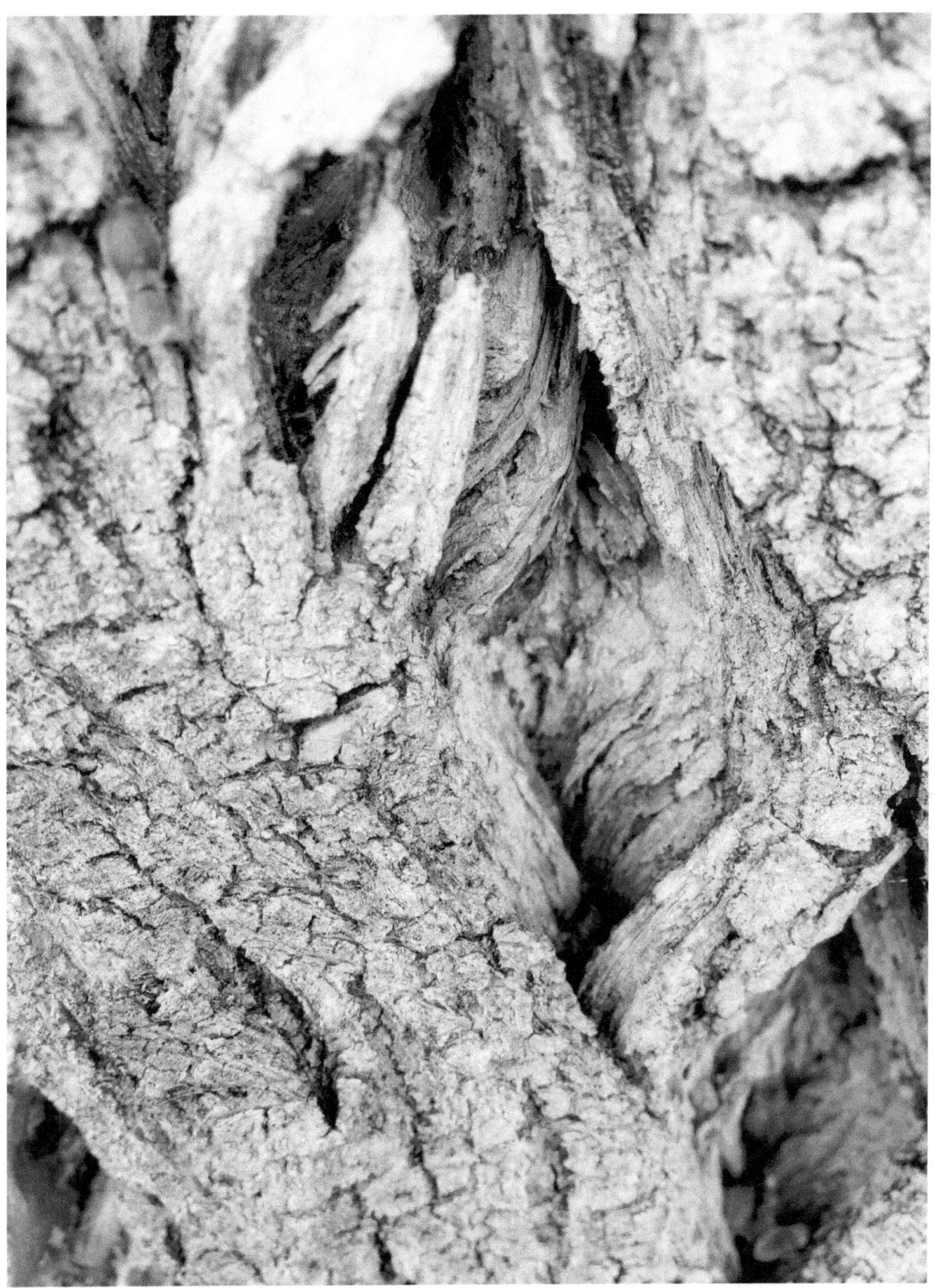

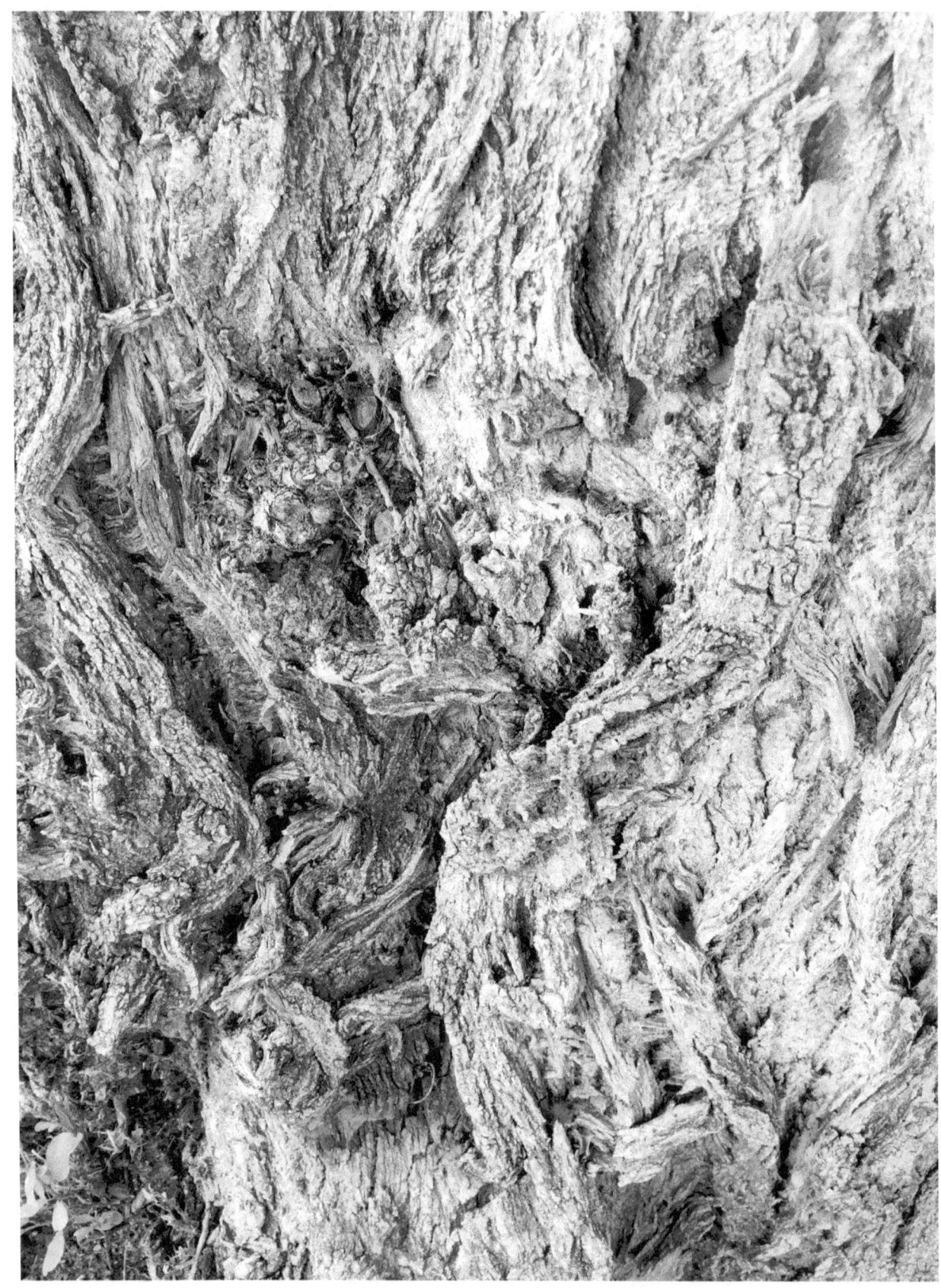

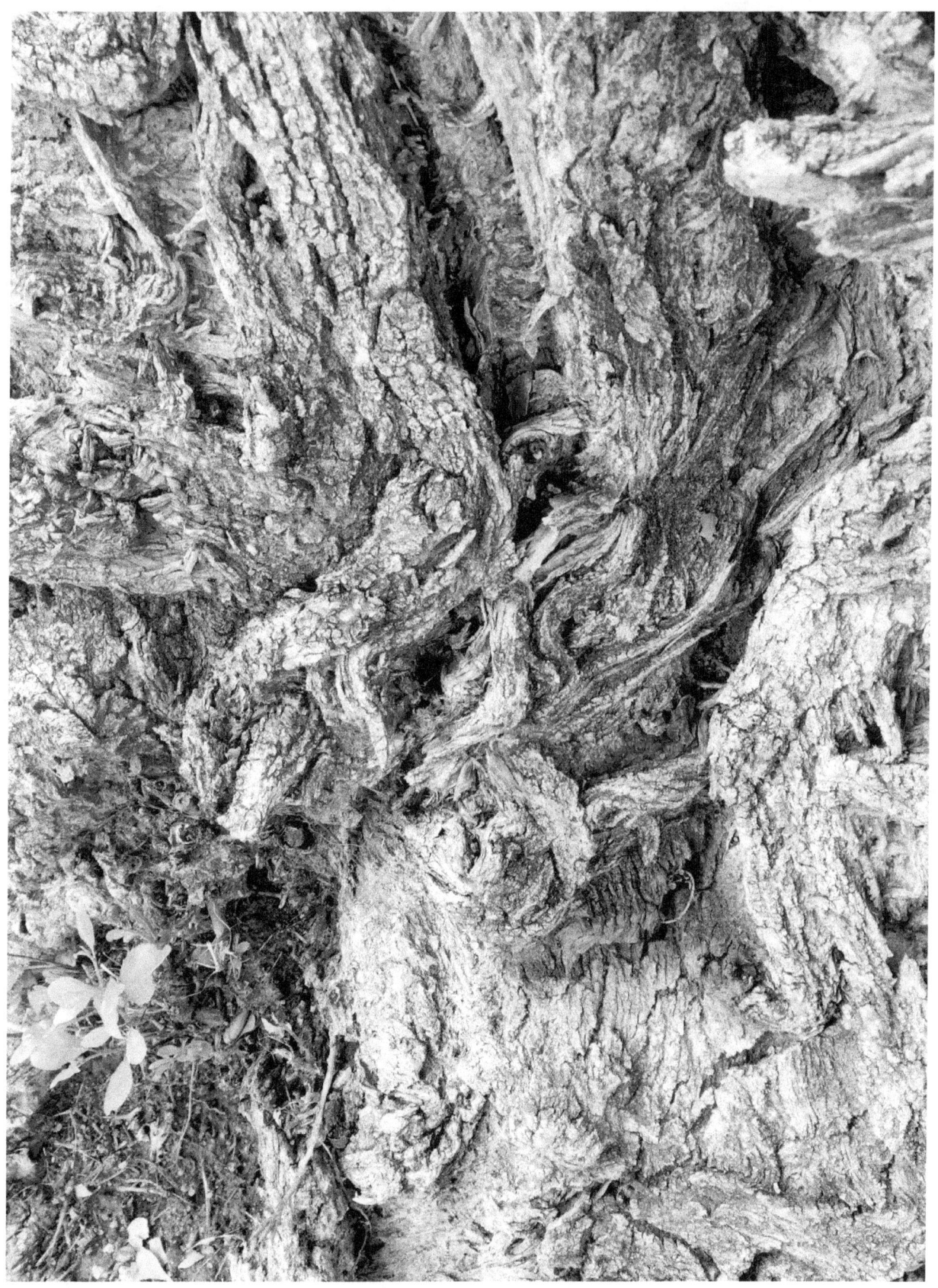

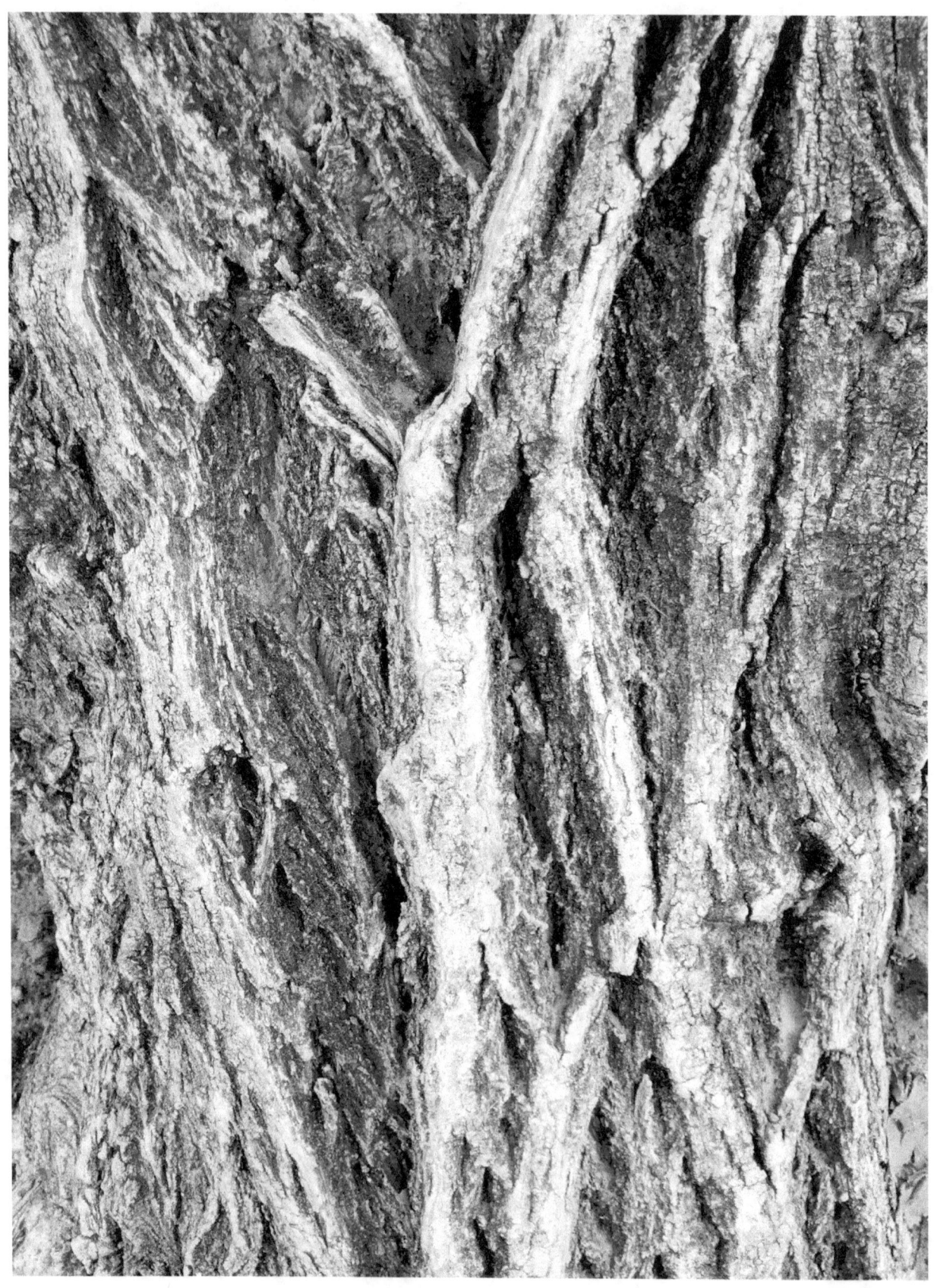

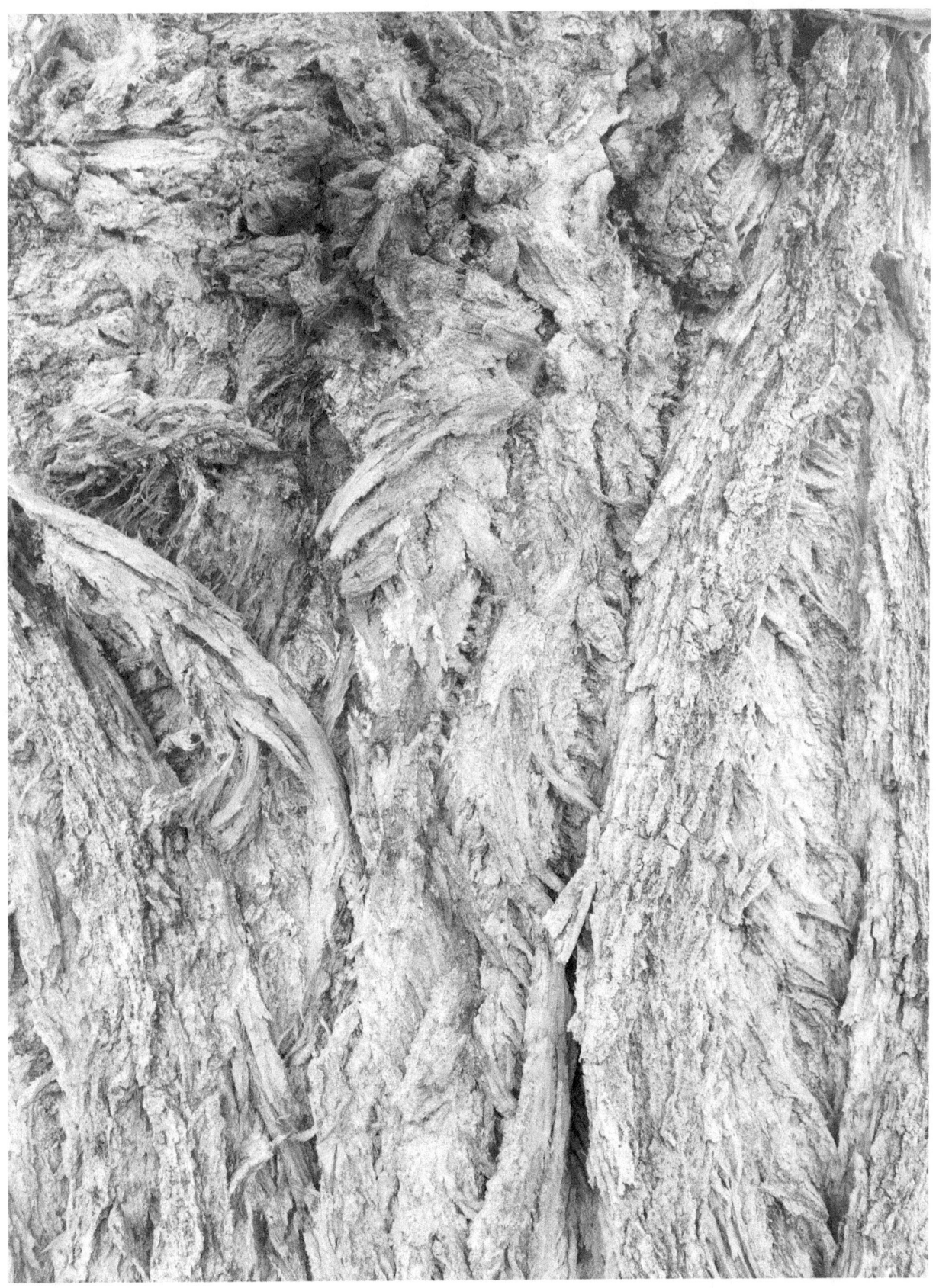

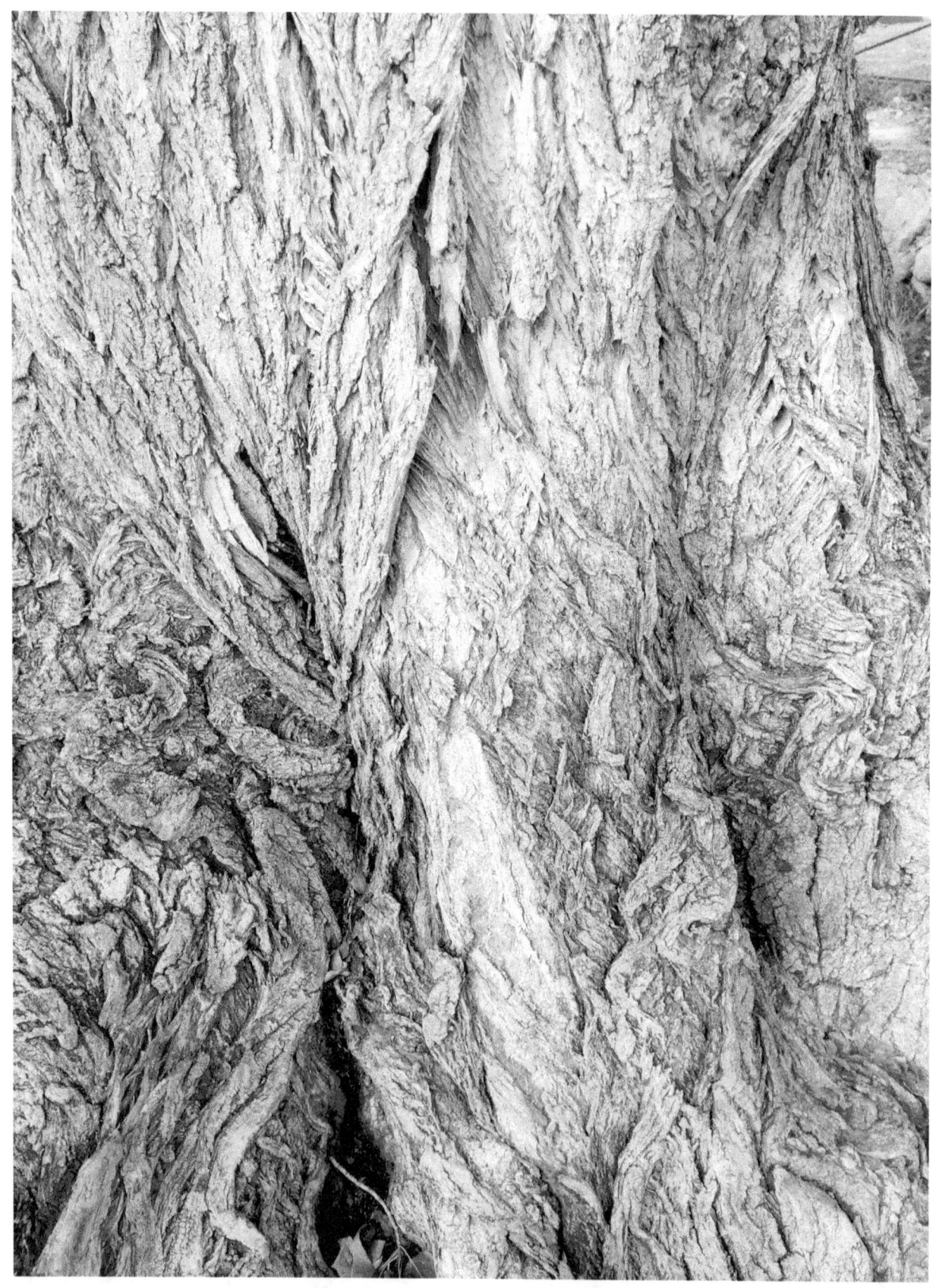

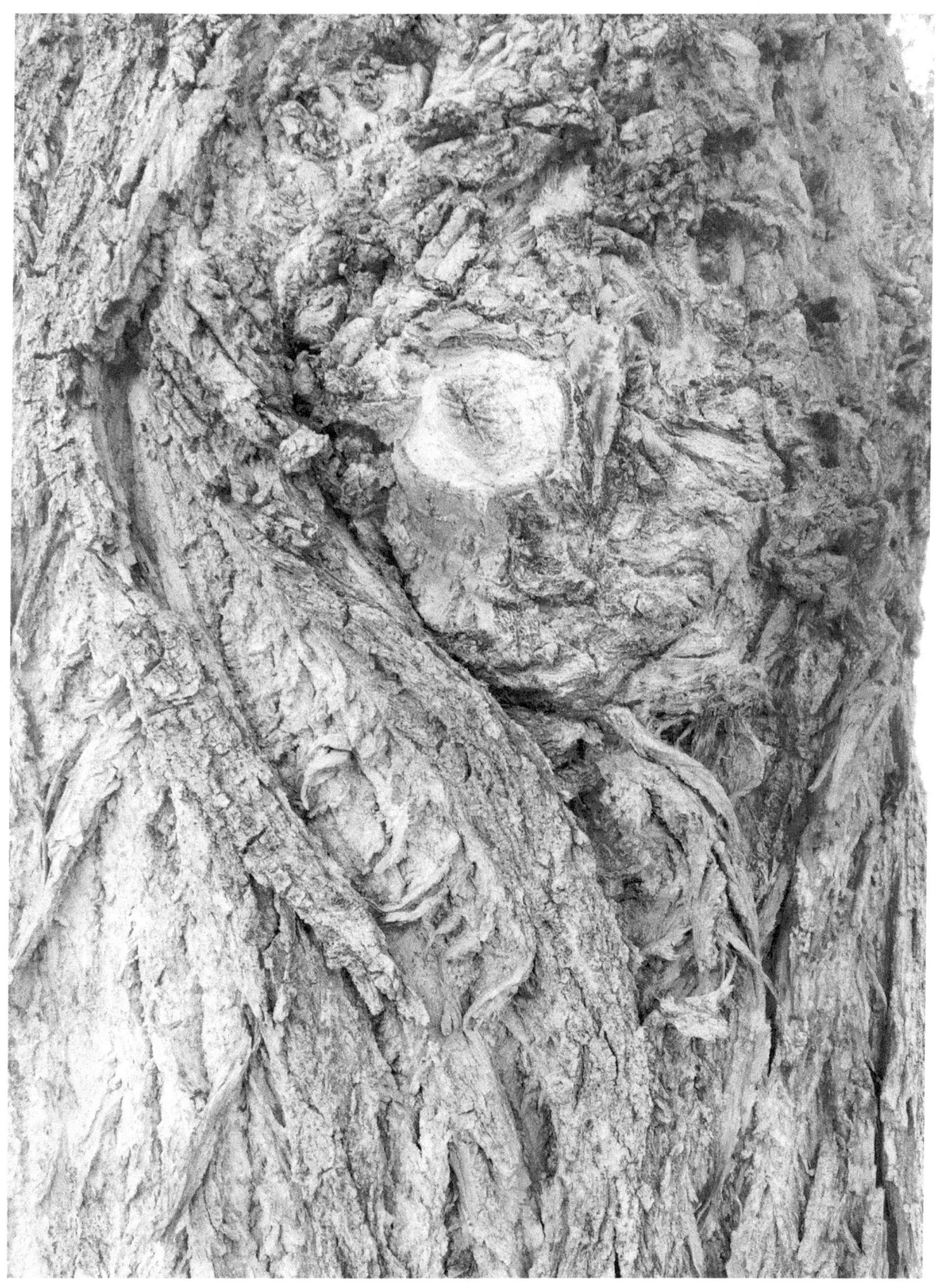

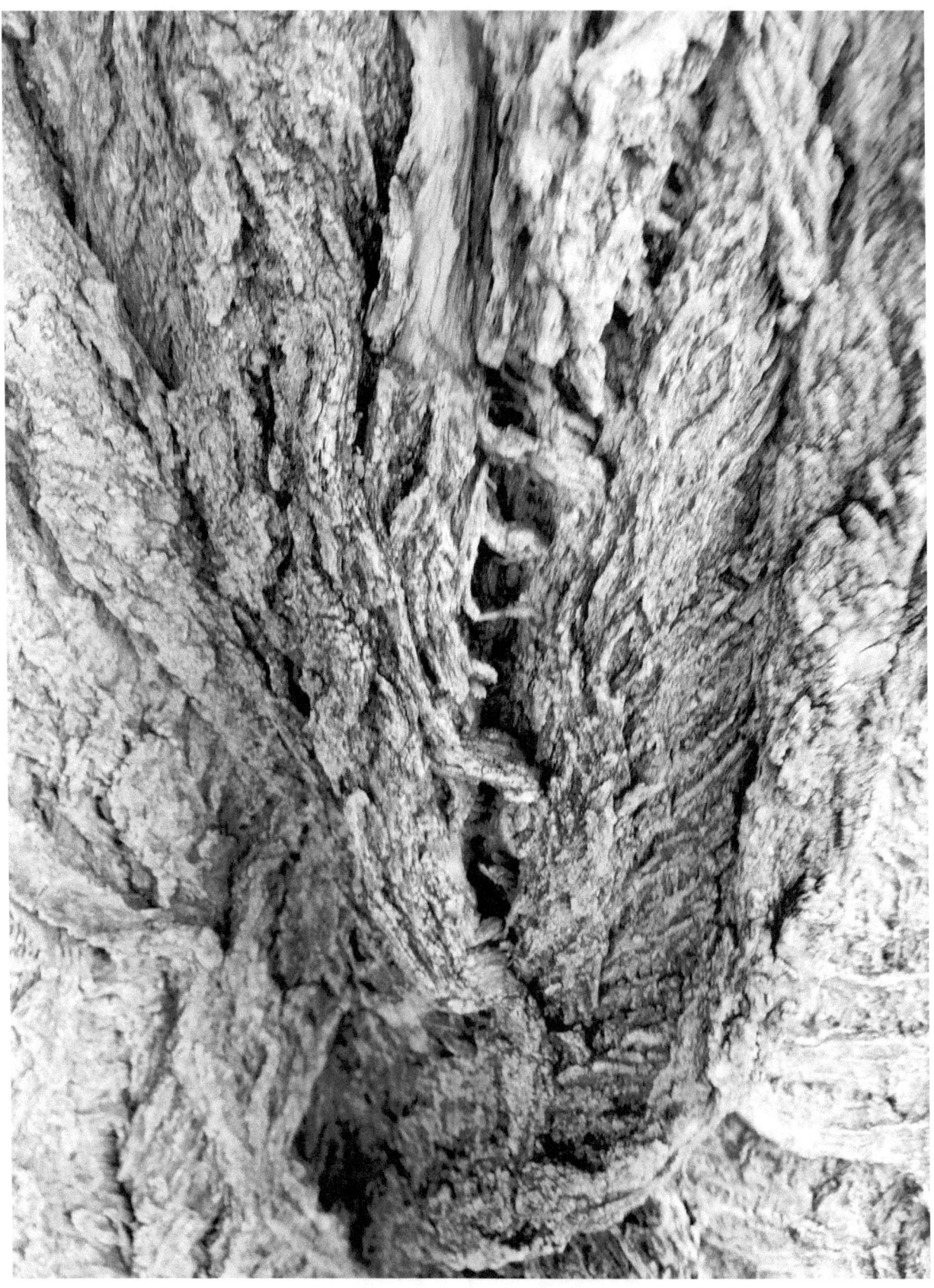

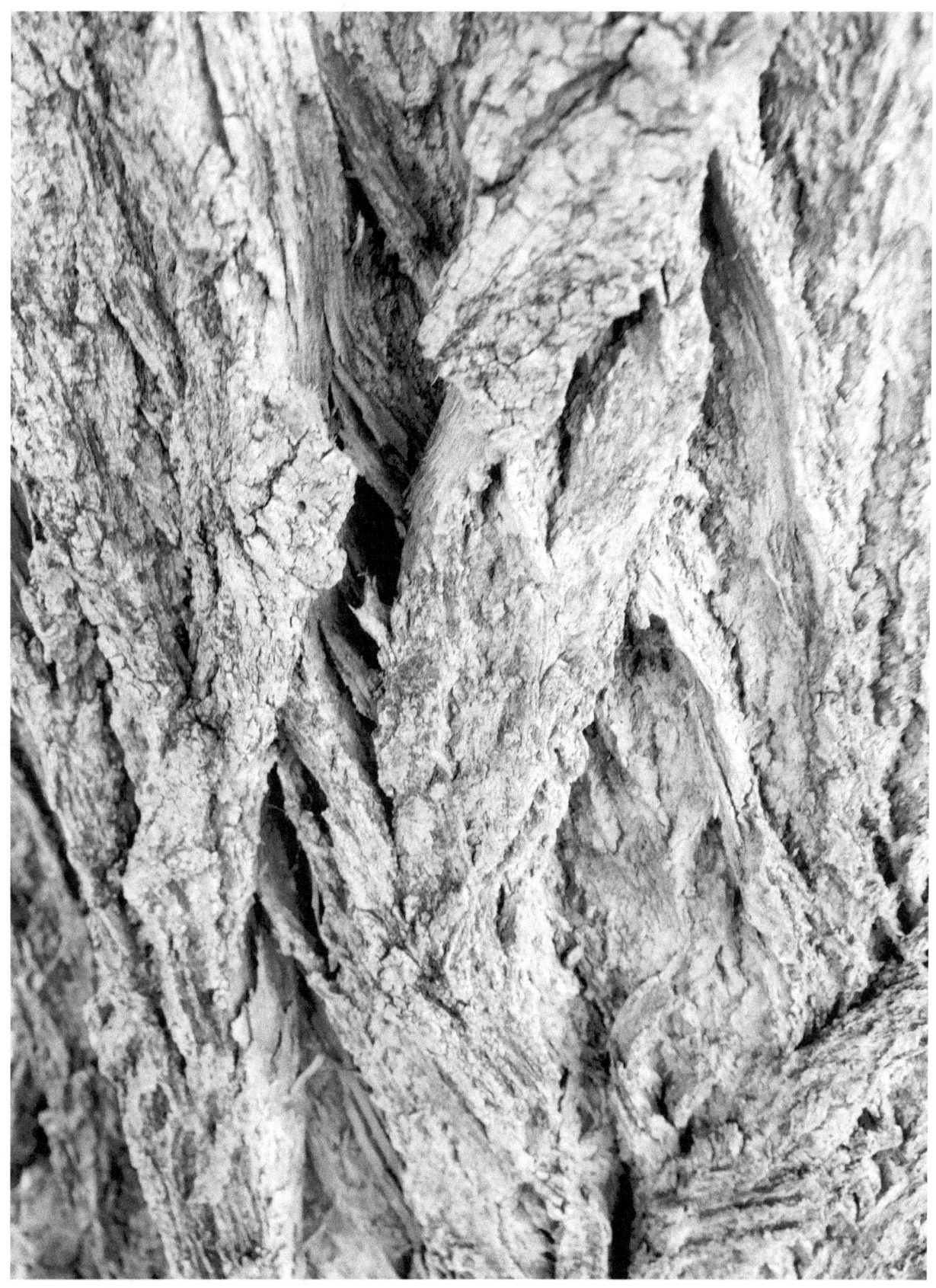

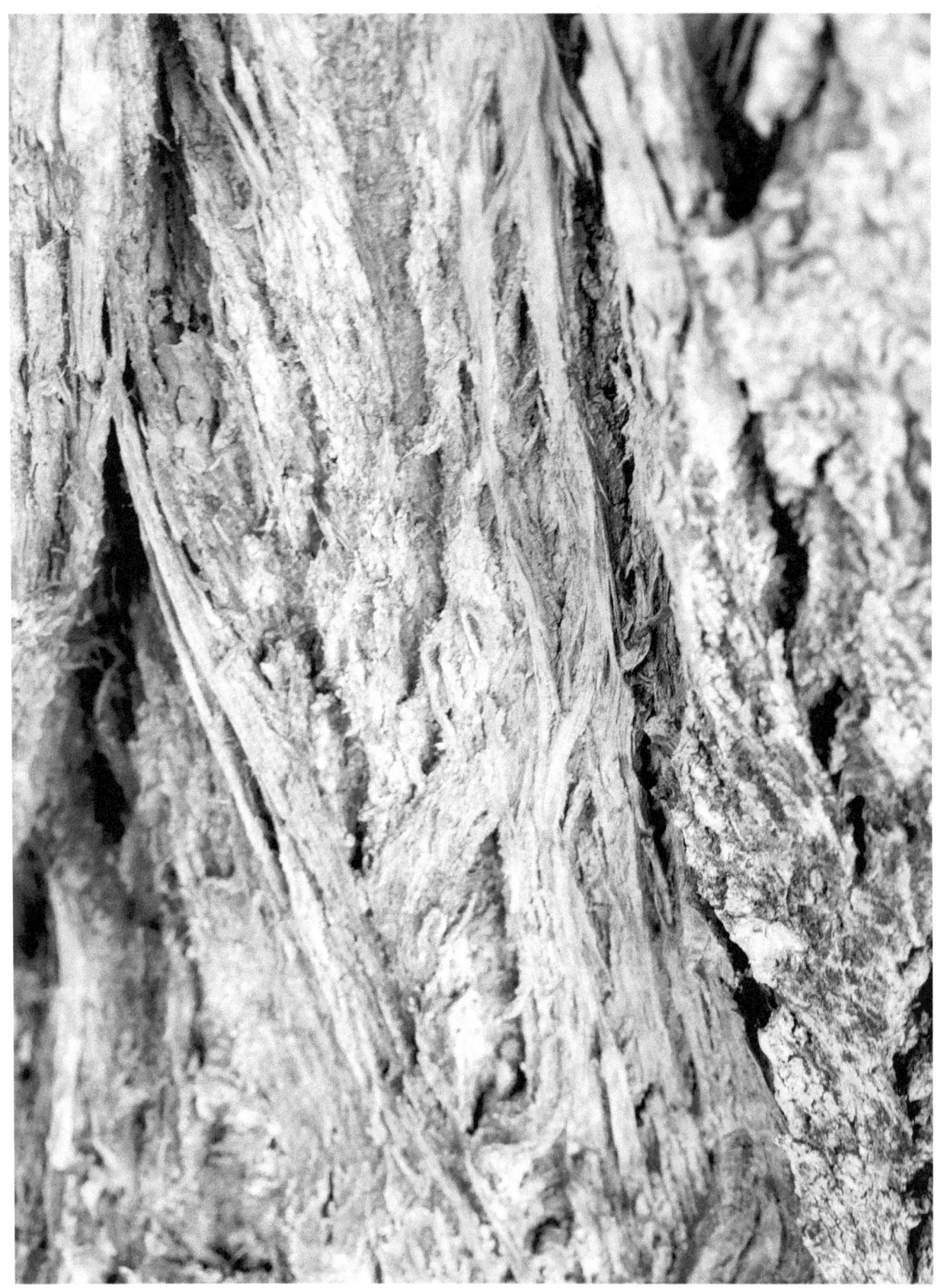